Warfare of the Believer

by
Richard Henton

Warfare of the Believer

by
Richard Henton

Vincom, Inc.
Tulsa, Oklahoma

Unless otherwise indicated, all Scripture quotations are taken from *The King James Version of the Holy Bible* (KJV).

Contents

1

The Warfare of the Saints

We have been taught in recent years that the devil belongs under our feet. Yes, he does — but it takes spiritual warfare to keep him there. Jesus defeated the devil and all of his works on the cross. (1 John 3:8.) However, that defeat must be *enforced* by the Church corporately and individually.

God is preparing His people in our day to do just that. Because he knows his time is very short, the devil has energized himself and is coming on strong in our day. He is operating through the entertainment media, through the music industry, and through society in general. That is why abortion was legalized, addicts of all types are increasing, and America in general is considered a ''post-Christian'' society.

The Church let him slip all of this over on us beginning in the late Fifties, and because of our negligence, now we are fighting a battle almost surrounded by the enemy in this country. The warfare God wants His people to understand is the battle to put the devil where he already *legally* belongs: under our feet.

The situation reminds me of a story about an airplane flight from Africa when a python being transported in a box got loose, and the men on the

1

plane were trying to put him back in his box. A python can have the strength of thirty men, so the guys on the plane were having difficulty getting the snake penned back up.

However, there was a man from Africa on the plane who knew how to handle snakes. He caught the python by the head and with one hand manuevered it back into the box and put a lid on it. Everyone on the plane knew the snake had been put in a box. They already knew he belonged in the box, but none of them had known how to get him there.

The devil knows where he belongs, and Christians know he was defeated by Jesus and "put in a box," so to speak. However, he is loose, and even few Christians know how to get him bound up and "in a box" as far as their lives are concerned.

The situation with the devil is like that with death, in that both have been defeated, but neither has been banished from our lives for good. Jesus defeated death on the cross, just as He defeated Satan. For the saints, when the body dies, life has really just begun. Death for the saints is like a "chauffeur." It transports us from here to there. At some future time, death will be banished for good, and our new bodies will never be subject to death.

At the Second Coming of Jesus, Satan will be bound for a thousand years, and later, he is to be put into the lake of fire forever. (Rev. 20:2,3,10.) In the meantime, we must defy him in our daily lives, and the Church should be defying him corporately.

Through faith, we must tell death, "You're not taking me until God is ready for me," and through faith in the name of Jesus, we must say, "Satan, you are not over me but under me."

The Apostle Paul wrote that our warfare is against the devil, not against flesh and blood. (Eph. 6:11,12.) However, demons are to be found where people are, not in wilderness or desert areas. Their main focus is to oppress, influence, or possess people, to live through them second-hand, and to stop or hinder the work of God.

Their assignments are to steal, kill, and destroy. The devil hates mankind, because Jesus as a man (having laid aside His divinity — Philip. 2: 5-8) defeated him. He has hated mankind since God prophesied in the Garden of Eden that "a seed of the woman" would bruise his head, and he would bruise the heel of the Seed. (Gen. 3:15.)

I heard a preacher say once that the reason Jesus' heel was bruised is because He "stomped" the devil's head so hard! The devil is so mad because he lost the fight. Now he is trying to pick on those of Jesus' people who are weak or lacking in knowledge enough to let him. He hates the Church today, because we are to enforce his defeat and put him and all of his troops in a box.

In any city or town, you will notice certain areas are more demon-infested than others. The more people live and work in ungodly ways, the more demons can exist in that place. There are becoming more and more of those places. I believe that, in times to come, it will take knowing God as a reality to be able to survive. I believe we have never seen spiritual warfare as we are going to see it in the next few years.

Christians in times to come are not going to have a lot of extra time on their hands to lounge around, be entertained, and indulge in small talk. The devil is going to be like a hound dog on our trails. A battle is going on, and Christians must be taught how to fight.

We do not know enough about the enemy's tactics. For example, you can read in the Bible that the devil quoted scriptures to Jesus (Matt. 4:1-11), but somehow we forget that he also can quote scripture to us. We must learn to discern what is God and what is not.

Also, we must learn that God does not always operate the same way. Sometimes, He fights the battles, and sometimes, we are supposed to fight them in His power.

In 2 Chronicles 20:15-17, the Lord told King Jehoshaphat that he and his army need not fight in that battle. He told them to "stand still" and see the Lord save them. Of course, all of the people were happy. But how long would they have lasted as a nation if they had assumed all the other battles from then on would be like that?

In verse 17, the Lord said, "You shall not need to fight in this battle."

In that battle, singers were appointed to praise and worship God while He won the battle.

When Israel took Jericho, they marched around the city once a day for six days and seven times on the seventh day, and then shouted! At that, the walls fell down. However, there were other battles under Joshua, David, and later kings of Israel and Judah, when the armies of the Lord's people had to fight the battles.

Whether the Lord fought or the people fought, however, they only won if they were in His will and fighting for His purposes.

Many Christians today operate as if what God said to Jehoshaphat was true for us in all areas.

They say things like, "The Lord fights my battles," and feel they do not have to do any warfare.

Sometimes you win battles by speaking; sometimes by knowing when to keep your mouth shut. But sitting down and saying, "I don't have to fight," will not put the python back in the box. He will just wind himself around you and squeeze you to death.

There are other battles that must be fought with prayer, battling in the spiritual realm with the deadly powers of darkness and the forces of hell. You must have wisdom to know how to fight the devil. You must know how to defend yourself when you are alone.

It is easy to get in church with everyone else and say, "Devil, we rebuke you in the name of Jesus. Get behind me, Satan!"

What will you do when you are out there by yourself and the enemy hits you with sickness, disease, losing your job, and so forth?

Christians need to learn how to defend themselves from spiritual attacks. This book is for those who want to go all the way with God, those who want to fulfill their chosen destinies.

This book is for those people who are doing something for God. The devil does not come after those who are not doing anything. They are no threat to him.

Some of God's people today are going to be put in places they never thought they would be, and they must be able to stand. He only puts people in hard places who He knows can stand the heat and deal with the devil. So instead of complaining about what you are going through, ask God to give you strength so that good can come out of those circumstances.

Christians do not always understand that when they became born again, they enrolled in an army, and that army requires steadfastness and spiritual strength. An army requires soldiers who are ready to fight.

Soldiers Must Be Ready To Fight

These are the days to be strong in what you believe, as Paul wrote to Timothy about the times in which they lived.

> Thou therefore, my son, be strong in the grace that is in Christ Jesus.
>
> And the things that thou hast heard of me among many witnesses, the same commit thou to faithful men, who shall be able to teach others also.
>
> Thou therefore endure hardness, as a good soldier of Jesus Christ.
>
> No man that *warreth* entangleth himself with the affairs of this life; that he may please him who hath chosen him to be a soldier.
>
> 2 Timothy 2:1-4

That is as plain as it can be. Paul warned Timothy not to be "entangled" with things of this life, and if it was true for Timothy, how much more for us in today's society. When you know that you have enlisted in God's army, you do not get involved in the affairs of the world as if they were permanent. You know that you are like Abraham and the other heroes of faith: strangers traveling through a strange land. (Heb. 11:13,14.)

God did not draft you; you were *chosen*. You were called, and you accepted the call. Some are called as privates, others as officers. But, whatever your "rank" in this army, each Christian has a place where he is to walk and assignments that only he can do.

Jesus fought a good fight before He ever went to the cross. The disciples and the early Christians fought a good fight. Paul, again writing to Timothy, said that he was ready to depart this life because he had *fought a good fight.* (2 Tim. 4:6,7.) Because of that, he was able to finish the race that had been set before him. He did everything he was called to do in this life.

Paul was opposed by the devil and his troops. They stirred up the crowds against him, attacked him with sickness, and even infiltrated the early churches to cause dissension and pull some off into false doctrines. Do you think that Paul did not fight the enemy? He fought the devil in prayer, in keeping his attitudes right, and in casting out demons wherever he could.

James said to resist the devil, and he would flee. (James 4:7.) *To resist* means to fight. You are to submit to God and resist the devil, but many Christians live the other way around. They submit to the attacks and influences of the enemy and resist God's call to stand up and fight.

No wonder the devil has been knocking down Christians. No wonder he has been standing on their heads, robbing them blind, and walking up the front and down the back of them. They have not been resisting him. You resist by prayer, by spiritual warfare (binding and loosing), and by standing against temptation in any area of your life.

You have to handle the devil the way you do a dog. You must make him mind as you would a dog, because that is all he is to you. But if you do not keep him down, he will jump on you. He lives on the ground, and you are walking tall with your head in the air. Yet you let him lick you in the mouth.

We need to put him down where he belongs. We need to be sober and vigilant. (1 Pet. 5:8,9.) The devil is out to destroy you. He has a warrant sworn out for your arrest, and he wants to take you out of the game. He wants to discourage you.

The first thing a Christian soldier needs to learn how to walk in the Spirit and not fulfill the lusts of the flesh. (Gal. 5:16,17.) That means walking in the will of God as witnessed to you by the Holy Spirit seven days a week. The devil does not mind you talking a good Christian talk in church, as long as you go home and live the rest of the week as if you never heard of Jesus.

Paul wrote that the flesh *lusts* against the spirit. That is a battleground right there! The flesh and the spirit man are contrary to one another. The Holy Spirit can be moving on you to pray "right now," and your flesh will tell you it is 3:30 a.m. The Spirit may be telling you to fast, but the flesh will remind you that you are having stomach problems. These things are contrary to one another.

You may think fashionable clothes and expensive cosmetics are the flesh. But you can take all the cosmetics off, use baking soda for deodorant, and exchange sheer nylons for thick black stockings. You can give up the expensive face creams and use vaseline, but when you get through with all that, *the flesh is still an enemy of God.*

There is something about your flesh that does not want to be subject to the Spirit. There is something in the soul that does not want to be subject to anyone else, even those being led by the God of our salvation.

Either Christ is on the throne, reigning as Lord over your life and self, and flesh is dying daily, receiving the "crucifixion with Christ," or flesh is rebelling against crucifixion. The "throne" of your life and the cross in your life must both be occupied rightly all the time: Jesus on the throne, and self on the cross. If you have that backwards, the devil can do pretty much what he wants to in your life.

If flesh says, "I'm not taking any more crucifying," and comes down off the cross, then Jesus humbly gets up off the throne and goes back on the cross. He is crucified anew while your flesh reigns on the throne. Those two places in your life — cross and throne — are never empty.

No house is big enough for two kings to sit on one throne. Flesh and Spirit cannot sit on the same throne. One has to give way to the other. Walking in the Spirit means being dead to self, dead to who you want to marry, dead to the profession or job *you* want to take, dead to sin — but alive to God and to His will in your marriage, job, and life.

God wants to make conquerors out of us.

We Are To Be More Than Conquerors

The Father wants to make conquerors out of us because He loves us. He wants us to win battles, not lose. He makes us conquerors through a series of steps that can be paralleled to joining the army in the natural.

When you are drafted into the armed services of the United States, the first thing they do is change your lifestyle. Instead of doing what *you* want to do, you must learn to obey orders. You must learn to submit to a higher authority. *You* are not in charge any longer.

The next thing they do in the services is change the way you look: civilian clothes for uniforms, fashion haircuts for regulation cuts, and so forth. The Lord has a "uniform" for us, as well. It is called "the whole armor of God," and I will discuss it in a later chapter in more detail.

I do not care what you have on that fits you and looks good, when you are inducted into the service, you will take off those clothes and put on what Uncle Sam says. However, many Christians do not put on the armor of God. They try to wear the old clothes of the old nature — and stay in trouble all of the time thereafter.

After you receive your uniforms, you undergo boot training. That is to cause you quickly to submit to authority, to cleanse out of you the sloppiness of doing your own thing, and to get you into good physical condition. Sometimes boot training is so rigid, especially in the Marines, that people have been known to have heart attacks because of the unaccustomed exertion.

Why do the officers do this to rookies? Are they mad at them? Do they hate them? No! They do this because they do not want them to get killed on the battlefield, and they do not want them to do stupid things that could cause someone else to get killed. Soldiers must be able to know how to crawl on their bellies with bullets whizzing by overhead if the occasion warrants. On the other hand, they must be able to instantly obey an order to charge the enemy head on, if that is the strategy on which the leaders decide.

Soldiers must know how to dig fox holes and how to lay in trenches full of water or wade through mud, if necessary. They must know how to go through barbed wire. To succeed, the soldiers-in-training must "lay aside every weight that so easily besets them." (Heb. 12:1.) A soldier must learn discipline.

Discipline means to be controlled, to train mentally, morally, and physically. Training sergeants will make recruits do things they do not want to do in order to break down that self-will and get them to the point where they can follow orders. In battle, that training could very well save their lives. It is for their benefit, not to be mean to them.

Troops are trained to operate in unity. Without unity, there would be chaos during the stress of battle. That training involves causing troops to drill in formation: ''Right face, left face, about face. Attention!'' Drilling means carrying out a systematic series of body movements to maintain order.

These regiments go in as individuals, but when the drill sergeant gets through with them, it looks like one pair of legs marching, not several dozen or more.

All of this is what God wants to do for Christians, but many of us end up being disobedient, rebellious soldiers whom God cannot use. If He sent us against the enemy, we would be wiped out. We have no personal discipline, no armor, no real commitment, and no unity. Also, many Christians have no idea what weapons they have, much less how to use them. And all of this information is written down in the ''Owner's Manual,'' the Bible.

Soldiers headed for battle must have a backpack, a canteen, camouflage gear, a rifle with a bayonet and ammunition, and field rations. Did you know a soldier must be able to take his weapon apart and put it back together in the dark?

Your weapon is the Word of God, the sword of the Spirit. You need to know it well enough to at least know what is in it. You may not know chapter and verse, but you can have an idea where a certain concept, principle, or commandment is found.

You can be able to say, ''That sounds like Psalms,'' or ''That sounds like Jeremiah,'' or Ezekiel, or the Apostle Paul.

Many Christians know these things, but somehow, the knowledge is not revelation. They agree mentally, but act as if it is not true. I believe from here on out, the Christian walk will be no vacation. I believe it is going to be warfare.

As spiritual warfare heats up, many Christians are sitting on the sidelines. The devil is destroying their faith, tormenting their minds, putting them into fear, and setting traps of temptation in front of their feet.

Evil men have crept in, as Jude wrote in his day, and it is time we "earnestly contend" for the faith once delivered to the saints. (v. 3.) Men are frustrating, trampling on, the grace of God, saying it is not wrong to kill unborn babies, commit adultery, or engage in perverse sexual acts.

Even in the Church, people are teaching that those things are okay. The grace of God has been changed to lasciviousness. If you do not know the Word in this day, you will be whipped. The only way to truly know God, know what He expects of you, and know the enemy is through the Bible.

Get in the Fight

It is time to get into the fight. You must know Heaven is your destination, but you do not want to let the devil shorten your life before God's use for you on earth is over.

To run the race until *your* course is finished, you must become as good a soldier as you possibly can. And you must understand that you will never make it in your own strength. You must be strong in the power of the Lord's might.

You must have offensive power as well as defensive.

Tell yourself, "I'm going to get on the firing line. I am going to move in where the action is. I am going to let God make a good soldier out of me for His purposes."

You want a new ministry? You must get in the fight. You want to operate in the gifts of the Spirit? You must get in the fight. You want to be anointed? You must fight to keep your anointing.

Satan is a defeated foe, yes, but he has not been destroyed. If you do not know he is defeated and act like it, he will operate in your life as if *he had never been defeated.* It is up to us to enforce the limits on him that Jesus gave us the power and the right to do.

By this time, I am sure you understand that I am not talking about physical warfare. When Jesus defeated the devil on the cross, it was not in natural warfare. Jesus did not fight those men of the Jews and Romans who were simply being used by the devil. He won over the devil by submitting to men and forgiving them.

It takes a lot of choosing to be like Jesus and a lot of practice in acting like Jesus before you can "fight" like that! Paul also wrote that, although we live in material bodies, we are not to fight in the natural.

> **For though we walk in the flesh, we do not war after the flesh.**
>
> **2 Corinthians 10:3**

Paul wrote that God had put all things under Jesus' feet and that death would be the final thing to come under the authority of Jesus. (1 Cor. 15:25-27; Eph. 1:22.) The last verses Paul wrote to the church at Rome include this promise:

And the God of peace shall bruise Satan under your feet shortly. . . .

Romans 16:20

That clearly proves that Satan is to be bruised under the feet of children of God, as well as under the feet of Jesus, the promised Seed. The devil and demons belong under the feet of the least of the saints, the smallest believer. We need to begin to put him where he belongs.

To do that, you must understand all of the different parts of the armor of God and how to use them.

2
The Armor of the Saints

I do not know any scripture more important to the born-again, Spirit-filled Christian than Ephesians 6:10-18:

> Finally, my brethren, be strong in the Lord, and in the power of his might.
>
> Put on the whole armour of God, that ye may be able to stand against the wiles of the devil.
>
> For we wrestle not against flesh and blood, but against principalities, against powers, against the rulers of the darkness of this world, against spiritual wickedness in high places.
>
> Wherefore take unto you the whole armour of God, that ye may be able to withstand in the evil day, and having done all, to stand.
>
> Stand therefore, having your loins girt about with truth, and having on the breastplate of righteousness;
>
> And your feet shod with the preparation of the gospel of peace;
>
> Above all, taking the shield of faith, wherewith ye shall be able to quench all the fiery darts of the wicked.
>
> And take the helmet of salvation, and the sword of the Spirit, which is the word of God:
>
> Praying always with all prayer and supplication in the Spirit, and watching thereunto with all perseverance and supplication for all saints.

Paul began this section of his letter to the Ephesians with the words *finally, my brethren.* That means these verses are not for everyone, only "the brethren," the people of God. Actually, all of Paul's fourteen epistles were written to the Church. Every epistle was written to exhort, to strengthen, to perfect the saints, and sometimes, to correct them. There were situations over which Paul had to rebuke the Christians in certain churches.

At times, he wrote to set the churches in order, to warn the people of possible false teachings or doctrines, of false teachers, and even of false Christians. Here, to the Christians at Ephesus, Paul ended his exhortations and guidelines for spiritual living with: **Finally, my brethren, be strong in the Lord, and in the power of his might** (v. 10).

Then he told them *how* to be strong in the power of the Lord's might. He told them to be strong in the power of the Lord's might, you must put on the *whole* armor of God.

Paul was saying, "You don't have to worry about failing as long as you keep that close relationship, that fellowship, with God."

Several years ago, an understanding about this hit me quite suddenly. I realized that, when Adam lost his fellowship with God through disobedience, *he also lost his place.* He was put out of the Garden of Eden. When you move out of that close fellowship with God, there is a spiritual place you lose — if you do not repent and get fellowship restored.

Adam could not do that, but praise the Lord, we can! We can repent and have fellowship restored in its fullness *because of Jesus.* Adam had no mediator to atone for his sins, nor did any of the early humans who lived. That is why God had to institute the Old

Covenant, in order for His people to have something like a "credit card" to use that would draw on the future atonement in order to restore fellowship, to be reconciled, with Himself.

Sin breaks fellowship with God, and if you lose that, you may not see that you have lost your spiritual place in the natural. Adam could see that he was put out of the Garden, which is a "picture" for us of what happens in the Spirit when a child of God breaks fellowship through disobedience of some kind.

Adam and Eve were still God's creation, and He still talked to the ones among their descendants who were turned toward Him all the way down through the years to Abraham. However, the close fellowship was gone, the place where God could come down "in the cool of the day" (Gen. 3:8) and walk with them. The place of mankind with God had been lost, until a covenant was made to restore fellowship temporarily.

Then Jesus came to restore fellowship *and* relationship permanently for all those who would receive His atonement.

So you may not notice in the natural that you have lost something of your spiritual place. You have not lost relationship, but fellowship, which places a barrier — or a spiritual distance — between you and the Father. You can still attend church, sing in the choir, praise the Lord, and pray. But you have moved out of that spiritual closeness to God.

Unless you get that restored, you will slip farther and farther away. It is not possible in the Christian life to remain in the same place. You either go forward or backward. And you must learn to battle temptations that would cause you to lose that fellowship. The enemy will do everything he can to get you to fall into various sins — even pride or anger, not just carnal sins.

That is why Paul wrote that Christians are soldiers. You cannot keep your fellowship with God without a battle with the enemy. Notice that Paul's letter to the Ephesians is placed in the Word *after* he had said we are more than conquerors through Him who loves us. (Rom. 8:37.)

The Holy Spirit inspired the men who made up the "canon" (the list and arrangement of books in the Bible by 367 A.D.) to place the admonitions to the Ephesians *after* Paul's epistle to the Philippians in which he wrote that he could do all things through Christ who strengthened him. (Philip. 4:13.)

All of Paul's letters were written specifically to groups of his time. We need to understand the context — social conditions, cultural environment, and so forth — in order not to misuse them and to apply them rightly to our own times. However, all of his teachings and his revealings of "mysteries" were for the benefit of all Christians through all time. I believe they are arranged in the order we need to study them, not necessarily in the chronological order in which they were written.

This warfare we are in is not just concepts or talk. It is *real*. The Christian walk is a fight until the body dies, and you go to be with the Lord. You will not need to fight the devil in Heaven. The battle already has been won there, and the devil cast out. But you are in a fight here on earth to the finish — and it is *your* finish that the devil wants.

Paul wrote Timothy to **fight the good fight of faith** (1 Tim. 6:12). Paul also looked back at the close of his own life and said:

> **I have fought a good fight, I have finished my course, I have kept the faith.**
>
> 2 Timothy 4:7

To fight does not mean simply "to stand in faith" holding on to what you have. *Fight* is not a passive verb, but an active one. It means "take action" against the enemy.

A Battle to the Death

The purpose of the armor is for you to be able to stand "in the evil day." If there were no evil days, you would not need the armor. However, all Christians must go through "evil days" in their own lives and in the conditions of society around them, from time to time.

You are in a life-or-death battle — a *real* battle. The devil is after your soul. He is no fool; he just tries to make fools out of us. The devil has no compassion, no mercy. He is an enemy who hates you with all the passion you can imagine. Also, he fights dirty. There is no point in getting into self-pity and feeling things "are not fair," because he does something to you. Of course, he is not fair. He uses every little loophole or "legal" technicality to hit you.

Without the armor of God and walking in the power of His might, you will not make it. The devil is merciless and a killer. However, with the armor of God and the authority of the name of Jesus, we have *all* power over all of his power. The point is: *We must make use of what we have,* or it will do us no good. We must enforce his defeat in our lives, or we will be defeated personally.

We need to stop fighting other people, especially our spouses and family members, and begin to fight the devil. If the devil is influencing or controlling someone, you could knock that person out and still do nothing to the demon, the source of their problems. You must get to the source.

You do not get to the source with sticks or bricks, or even arguments and persuasions. You must get to the source through the supernatural power of God. Usually, however, we do not want to fight that way. If Jesus had given us straight razors and told us to cut the devil's throat if he bothered us again, Christianity would be the biggest army in the world!

Even the disciples had that attitude. When the soldiers came to take Jesus, Peter cut off the right ear of one of them. (John 18:10.) Peter would not have denied Jesus if he could have fought with natural weapons. He would have fought to the death. But the devil hit Peter with fear, and he did not fight the good fight of faith. He caved in, and denied Jesus.

Peter found that you must put up your natural weapons. He found out that the soldiers were not the enemies — the devil was. When Peter moved into spiritual warfare, he did not have what it took. I am afraid many of us today are in the same place. When the devil throws up his heavy artillery, many Christians have tried — and will try — to fight the people involved, instead of using spiritual weapons to deal with the situation.

The devil has set out to do in America what the Soviets did in Hungary before they took them over. First, they came in and confiscated all their weapons. Then they walked in and took over without a real fight. The people had nothing to fight with. Today, the devil has set out to do the same thing.

He took prayer out of schools and God out of government. Then he took moral restraints off the entertainment industry — and the Church has allowed it to happen. Instead, the devil promoted material goods, greater things to do "for fun," and what seemed like greater prosperity.

Even the churches have prospered, with better and bigger buildings. Now, there is nothing wrong with building what God has told you to build. But we need to not ever forget that "the Church" is the people, not the buildings in which they meet.

When the devil thinks he can win, he will pull the prosperity out from under this country. Then Christians will have to find out if they still are in that fellowship place with God enough to know what to do. Then they will find, like Peter, whether they will resort to natural weapons or even to denial of Christ.

We must learn spiritual combat. We must learn how to overcome when we are alone. You need to learn how to "bear your own burden" in case you cannot find anyone else to stand with you. Paul said to "be strong in the Lord," not strong in your church, or strong in your family. We are wrestling against satanic powers, not people.

This spiritual battle we are in is more serious than the Civil War, the Revolutionary War, or the World Wars. The most that could happen in those wars was that the body could be killed. This war can cause the spirit to be "killed" in hell. *Real* death, which a true Christian will never face, is to be eternally separated from God.

Think about a natural wrestling match. You see two men, one trying to subdue the other. Two powers are matched. That is what we are involved in: Enforcing the power of good over the power of evil. Yes, I cannot say too often that Jesus defeated the devil, *but he is not yet destroyed*. God left something for us to do. In our strength, we could not defeat the devil. But through Jesus already giving him the "knock-out punch," we can climb into the ring and finish him off.

God wanted us to have a part in His purposes and plans.

Sometimes I have lain down at night, and one demon after another has appeared before me. Every one of them looks different, and none of them is pretty. But I do not get afraid. I know the strength of my God and the power of His might. I know the armor I wear.

I just say, "Demons, you are all liars. Whatever your purposes are, in Jesus' name, you are not going to accomplish them. Now, git!"

The devil has more demons than you can count. All of them do not look like human beings. All of them do not look like rats, snakes, frogs, turtles, cats, and so forth. Some look like moss; some look like "chitlin's." There are demons that look like everything — all with eyes.

You need to know your armor, piece by piece, and in detail.

Know the Various Pieces of Your Armor

Starting from the head, look at the different pieces of armor that Paul listed.

He said to take "the helmet of salvation." *Salvation* means deliverance, and the purpose of a helmet is to protect the head from attacks. The *head* is the communications center, just as the spirit man is supposed to be the "control and command center." Without the head being under authority — protected by salvation — the commands from the Spirit would not go forth to the body or the soul (mind, will, and emotions).

Therefore the first thing a Christian must know is that he, or she, is *saved*. He must wear the knowledge of his salvation as a helmet. His sins are covered. He is under the protection and covering of the Lord Jesus Christ. The blood of Jesus makes up the helmet. It covers the ''doorposts'' — the eyes, ears, mouth, and brain centers that issue commands to the rest of the body.

The next vital part to be covered is the chest area, the place where the heart is located. God has given us a ''breastplate of righteousness.'' Our own ''righteousness'' is as filthy rags, but Jesus took ours and imparted His to us. He ''covered'' us with His righteousness.

If you are hit in the arm or leg, you can survive. But if you get hit in the chest, you may not. That is why SWAT teams of police wear bulletproof vests.

In addition to the breastplate, God has given us ''the shield of faith.'' Faith is something we can ''move around'' to whatever area needs protecting.

The next vital area is the loins. Paul said to gird them about with *truth*. Where do you get truth? You get it from studying the Word. For example, if you know the *truth* from God's Word concerning marriage and the marriage relationship, the devil will not be able to tempt you with lust.

The loin cloth also was the place where the dagger was kept. If a soldier in Paul's day had a battle ax, a dagger, or a sword, it was fastened in the top of his girdle. Battles then were fought with strength more than strategy, so a soldier needed to have a two-edged sword handy to swing both ways against the enemy.

You must have the truth of the Word of God wrapped around you. That is where your offensive weapon comes from.

The last piece of defensive armor is "the gospel of the preparation of peace" for your feet.

When Scripture says "have your feet shod," the mental image from the Greek word was of shoeing horses in a blacksmith shop. That means you do not take them off. The "good news" (gospel) that God has been at peace with man since Jesus rose from the dead (Col. 1:20) should be so much a part of us that it is as if we actually had that truth fastened to our feet.

The majority of mankind still is not at peace with God and that will have to be dealt with at the Second Coming. However, Jesus paid the price for mankind's original disobedience and for all sins. So God is at peace with us — if we will be at peace with Him. (John 16:33.) That means staying in fellowship.

The footwear of soldiers in Paul's day involved more than the sandals we see in pictures. They had brass shinguards attached to the shoes as well, in order to protect the fronts of their legs from the instep on up to the knees.

More than that, the "gospel of the preparation of peace" means walking in peace with all men insofar as is possible. (Rom. 12:18; 2 Cor. 13:11; Heb. 12:14.) Jesus wanted His disciples to be known as *His*, because of the way they loved one another. (John 13:34,35.) Therefore, members of the Body of Christ must let the world see that we are different because we walk in peace with one another, regardless of race, gender, or even doctrinal differences (those who do not involve the basics of the faith).

Peace is to be our spiritual combat boots.

Paul's picture of the armor of God was based on what soldiers wore in his day. His readers could understand it, because they saw such "uniforms" almost every day in their streets. If you will notice, most of what Paul wrote concerning armor in Ephesians is *defensive* armor. The offensive part involves weapons *against* the enemy. Even most Christians who have understood the armor of God have used defensive armor more than offensive.

In the early Church, when active persecution was rampant, or in Iron Curtain countries since World War I, what Christians have needed is offensive armor, as well as defensive. I believe that is what all Christians will need in the days to come.

It will not be enough to have a strong defense, to know how to stand your ground. You will need a strong offense as well. You need also to be trained in the use of your offensive weapon. If you are not trained, you will be knocked out the first time you get in the ring.

Fighters must be trained. Christian soldiers must know when to bind and when to lose, when to resist your adversary the devil and when to agree with your human adversary (Matt. 5:25), when to talk and when to hold your peace, and when to stand your ground and when not to. You must know when to "roll with the punches."

Your enemy is a "long-distance" fighter. He will retreat today in order to win tomorrow. To stand, you must be trained in how to maintain the defensive armor whole and operational at all times. Then you must know how to use your defensive armor: how to wield the shield of faith so that the enemy's fiery darts are quenched and how to use the sword of the Spirit.

Faith has the ability not only to deflect the darts of the enemy so that they fall at your feet, but to quench them so they fall lifeless at your feet. There is no "fire" left in them to trip you up later.

The sword of the Spirit has won more battles, bound more demons, raised more people from the dead, and healed more sick than we could number. It is a powerful weapon. You need to study the Word of God enough to have it hidden in your heart, as David said. (Ps. 119:11.)

The devil is always going to seemingly come out of nowhere and challenge you to a duel. Whether it is sickness and disease he tries to put on you, accidents, loss of jobs, goods, and money, or whatever else in life, it presents a challenge. If you look on it as the enemy challenging you to a duel, you can come out swinging and defeat him. If you look at those things as "natural" calamities that you can do nothing about, you will lie down under them.

You must learn to defend yourself in a corner, as well as in open spaces. The enemy does not always give you warning.

Paul wrote that our weapons are not "carnal," which means of a material nature. They are not natural, but mighty through God to the pulling down of strongholds. In the next chapter, I want to discuss the Christian's offensive weapons in more detail.

3
Weapons Against Strongholds

In Ephesians 6:17, Paul told us the offensive weapon of the Christian is **the sword of the Spirit, which is the word of God.** In 2 Corinthians 10:3-5, Paul wrote why we are to use the sword of the Spirit and not try to fight spiritual enemies with natural weapons.

> For though we walk in the flesh, we do not war after the flesh:
>
> (For the weapons of our warfare are not carnal, but mighty through God to the pulling down of strong holds;)
>
> Casting down imaginations, and every high thing that exalteth itself against the knowledge of God, and bringing into captivity every thought to the obedience of Christ.

This is not physical warfare, but spiritual. Our weapons are mighty through God, Paul wrote. He told us of *one* weapon associated with the armor of God, but there are others mentioned elsewhere that we will look at in this chapter as well.

What does the Bible tell us about the sword of the Spirit? Look at Hebrews 4:12:

> The word of God is quick, and powerful, and sharper than any two-edged sword, piercing even to the dividing asunder of soul and spirit, and of the joints and marrow, and is a discerner of the thoughts and intents of the heart.

Jesus dueled with Satan after He came out of the forty-day fast in the wilderness at the very beginning of His ministry. Jesus won that battle, and the Bible says that Satan "departed from him for a time." (Luke 4:13.) At that time, Jesus had not whipped the devil, and you notice Satan only departed "for a season," which means "for a while."

That is what he does with us, even when we whip him with the Word. Sooner or later, you have to do it again to keep him in his rightful place under your feet. But how can you whip him with the Word when you do not know it?

The devil *knows* Scripture. He quoted it to Jesus but twisted it into meanings not intended, and Jesus was able to answer him with words and correct meanings from the Old Testament. Jesus *understood* the scriptures, not because He was God, but because He had studied the books of the Old Testament as a little Jewish boy in Nazareth.

Jesus learned the Word of God as a human being, just as you and I have to. You must "sharpen" your sword, which means you must know the Word well, if you are going to use it against the enemy.

One of the things Jesus said to Satan was . . . **Man shall not live by bread alone, but by every word of God** (Luke 4:4). Jesus was quoting Deuteronomy 8:3, and He knew the Word by heart. He had no scroll with Him in which to look up an appropriate verse. Nor will you always have a Bible handy in which to hunt the right verse on which to stand or to use against the devil.

Also, you sharpen your sword by placing faith in the Word. You take the Word as a sword in order to defeat the devil. Notice that Jesus Himself did not fight the devil with *who* He was. Every time the devil came at Him with a temptation, Jesus came back with the Word.

He did not say, "Devil, I threw you out of Heaven. Don't you know who I am? How dare you try to tempt Me!"

When the devil dared Him, "If you really are the Son of God, command these stones to be transformed into bread," Jesus accepted the battle and pulled out His "sword." Then the devil tried it again, actually daring Jesus to throw Himself off the temple and prove He was God by having the angels catch Him.

Jesus took up His sword and backed the devil off with a rebuke, **It is said, Thou shalt not tempt the Lord thy God.** Jesus and the devil were "fencing" on the pinnacle (the highest point) of the temple in Jerusalem, and Jesus was using a two-edged sword.

When a fencer lets his opponent know the match is about to begin, he says *En garde* (French for "on guard"). In other words, "Get ready to fight. Defend yourself. I'm about to attack." We should know the devil says that to us as soon as we become born again.

However, in Bible days, a soldier did not simply thrust his sword into someone and pull it out nice and clean. They were trained to thrust in the sword, then twist it, so that both sides cut into the opponent. A two-edged sword could indeed divide joints from marrow!

That is what Jesus did to the devil, and that is what we need to do. The devil was so wounded he turned tail and fled, although he was not yet defeated. Jesus did not have a scratch. He was only hungry from the fast, and when He had chased off the devil, angels came and ministered to Him.

Some Christians only want to be protected. They pray for God to be a fence around them, a wall of fire.

I believe God is saying, "Get on out where the action is. Every time I look at you, Church, you are in trenches, hiding behind stuff, or yelling for Me to come get you out of things. Put your bayonets on those rifles. Get out the two-edged sword, and go out against the enemy. Is this the *rock* on which Jesus planned to build the Church?"

We need to be like one of David's mighty men, who fought the Philistines. The Bible says he held his sword so tightly in battle that his muscles had become paralyzed, and his hand was locked to the sword.

> **And after him was Eleazar the son of Dodo the Ahohite, one of the three mighty men with David, when they defied the Philistines that were there** (at the battle at Pasdammim, 1 Chron. 11:13,14) **gathered together to battle, and the men of Israel were gone away;**
>
> **He** (Eleazar) **arose, and smote the Philistines until his hand was weary, and his hand clave unto the sword: and the Lord wrought a great victory that day; and the people returned after him only to spoil.**
> **2 Samuel 23:9,10**

That is how we should be. We must become one with the Word. Whatever the Word says, we must say the same thing.

Imaginations, Strongholds, High Things, and Thoughts

Before we take our swords out *after* the devil, Paul was telling us to use the sword of the Word against any ground the devil has *in* us. What are the imaginations, strongholds, high things, and thoughts that he was talking about?

Imaginations are those things the mind conjures up that are not real. Fantasies, delusions, and illusions can range from seemingly harmless daydreams to evil scenarios in which you see yourself killing someone. Many people, even Christians, live in a "fantasy world" in a manner of speaking. They twist things in their minds to suit themselves, to make themselves comfortable, and to avoid facing reality.

Fear can trigger imaginations; lust can trigger them; pride and ambition can trigger them. All of those emotions are *strongholds*, places in your mind where the devil has a right to roost. You cannot wield the sword of the Spirit if there is "dead flesh" attracting vultures.

Stop imagining so much. If you do not know something is a fact, cast it down. Imaginations stemming from jealousy have caused many tragedies, not to speak of simple misery in relationships. Jealousy is crueler than the grave (Song of Sol. 8:6), and it will give you a heart attack if it does not push you into something you always would regret. Cast down those thoughts before they can cast you down.

When the devil can defeat you in your own mind, he does not have to go any farther. Fits of depression are attacks of the enemy, and they attack the mind and the emotions. If he can keep you condemned over things in your past that you have repented of — and God has even forgotten (anything under the blood is wiped out of God's book) — then he can keep you defeated.

You need to get over those old sins and mistakes, or you will never get past them. The old saying that you cannot keep birds from flying over your head, but you can stop them from making a nest in your hair is very true. You *can* bring those thoughts into captivity.

High things are philosophies and beliefs that exalt themselves against God: humanism, false religions, atheism, agnosticism, and so forth. Compare everything you believe with the Word, and throw out what does not fit with it.

As for *thoughts,* sometimes you must resist them, and sometimes you must wrestle with the devil half the night:

"Devil, you are a liar. I am claiming what God has said. Devil, you are defeated."

Too many Christians fight two minutes and then give up exhausted, out of spiritual breath, out of faith, out of courage, and out of power. You have to build up spiritual strength. You must "hang in there" until you win.

Quote the Word, and just like the snow or rain falling gently to the earth, it will accomplish something. The Word will convict, save, heal, and bring deliverance. All of those things defeat Satan. God said that He watches over His Word to perform what He says. (Isa. 55:11.) Also, He said in the same verse that His Word will not return unto Him void. That means "empty" or without effect.

The Word will bring to pass what God pleases. It will go out convincing, saving, healing, defeating the devil, and come right back to His feet, having accomplished what He intended.

So quote the Word to yourself. Pull down those imaginations, throw out all those beliefs you gained from public school and television that are contrary to the Word, and repent of strongholds. Allow the Holy Spirit to cleanse your mind of negative emotions, unforgivenesses, anger, and so forth.

Then, every time a thought comes to you that is not in line with the Word of God, take it "into captivity" and get rid of it.

The devil likes to keep you sad and depressed, feeling downtrodden and oppressed. He uses those strongholds set up in the past — "my daddy had a temper, his daddy had a temper, so I have to have a temper" — to take control of your thoughts and beat you through your own mind.

You *believe* you cannot control your temper, for example, because "it runs in the family." That is a stronghold of the enemy. The blood of Jesus is stronger than any belief like that; it is stronger than anything — like diabetes — that *really* is inherited in the genes and passed down through the generations.

If His blood can heal those inherited diseases, it certainly is strong and powerful enough to cleanse out all those things you only *think* you have to do. You are a child of the King of the universe. You are not supposed to go around looking as if you had just bitten into an unripened persimmon or an extra-sour pickle.

The devil is defeated, and you have to know he is and be able to keep him reminded of it. Look at Ephesians 1:19-23:

> And what is the exceeding greatness of his power to usward who believe, according to the working of his mighty power,
>
> Which he wrought in Christ, when he raised him from the dead, and set him at his own right hand in the heavenly places,
>
> Far above all principality, and power, and might, and dominion, and every name that is named, not only in this world, but also in that which is to come:

And hath put all things under his feet, and gave
him to be the head over all things to the church,

Which is his body, the fulness of him that filleth
all in all.

Paul wrote that we must believe in the "exceeding
greatness" of God's power toward us who believe. The
power of God raised Jesus from the dead and set Him
at His own right hand — for us, and so that God's
purposes in creating man could be fulfilled. He set
Jesus *far* above all other powers and authorities and
above every name.

In order to make it perfectly plain, Paul added that
God has put *all things* under the feet of Jesus. God set
Jesus as head over all of the people who make up the
Body of Jesus, the "fullness" of Him.

You may think, "Look where Jesus is. He deserves
that place, but it has nothing to do with me."

Look again: The devil is not up there above Jesus.
He is not even above us. We are seated with Jesus in
heavenly places, because *we are His Body*. We are "the
fullness of Him." God designed us to work with Jesus
as Lord and King, together in a corporate oneness
simply because He loved us. That means *we* also are
above the devil.

But God, who is rich in mercy, for his great love
wherewith he loved us,

Even when we were dead in sins, hath quickened
us together with Christ, (by grace ye are saved;)

And hath raised us up together, and made us sit
together in *heavenly places in Christ Jesus:*

That in the ages to come he might shew the
exceeding riches of his grace in his kindness toward
us through Christ Jesus.

Ephesians 2:4-7

Other Weapons of the Saints

In addition to the Word of God, the sword of the Spirit, the Lord provided other ways in which we can keep the devil under our feet. Those include the name of Jesus, the blood of Jesus, praise and worship, prayer, fasting, the power of the Holy Spirit, angels, being in agreement, and then one most Christians may not think about — stillness — His peace. Also, the anointing of the Holy Spirit is a weapon.

The sword of the Spirit was a weapon even to those living under the Old Covenant. But the first weapon God gave us after Jesus rose from the dead was the *name* of Jesus.

In Mark 16:15-18, what is called "the Great Commission," Jesus said, "**In my name** you will do all these things. You will heal the sick, cast out demons, and speak with new tongues."

You can see all through the book of Acts that the disciples caught hold of this weapon immediately. They began to heal and cast out demons "in the name of Jesus."

The Pharisees and the high priest who arrested Peter and the other disciples at the temple interrogated them concerning the healing of the man lame from birth.

They asked, **By what power, or by what name, have ye done this?** (Acts 4:7). And Peter answered boldly:

> Be it known unto you all, and to all the people of Israel, that by the name of Jesus Christ of Nazareth, whom ye crucified, whom God raised from the dead, even by him doth this man stand here before you whole.
>
> **Acts 4:10**

Peter had put away his natural sword and picked up his spiritual weapons. In his discourse before the high priest, he continued to use the name of Jesus and the sword of the Spirit. He quoted scriptures to them. There was power in the name of Jesus then, and there is power in it now.

Not only the name of Jesus, but His blood is a weapon. In Revelation 12:11, it says the saints overcame by their testimonies and the blood of Jesus. Praising God is a weapon against the enemy. Demons do not like to hear you genuinely praising the Lord, and they certainly do not like to hear talk about the blood of Jesus. His blood is what defeated their master, Satan.

When Paul and Silas were in jail, beaten, bleeding, and fastened in chains, they praised the Lord at midnight — and an earthquake loosened their chains and shook the doors of the prison open. (Acts 16:25,26.)

You must be able to praise God in the middle of everything. (1 Thess. 5:18.) That pushes back the demons around you.

You must learn how to say, and *mean*, ''Devil, I come against you in the name of Jesus. The blood of my Lord and King cries out against you. I come against you because it is written that He that is in me is greater than he that is in the world (1 John 4:4) — and that's *you*, devil!''

In that one paragraph of coming against the devil, you have used three weapons: His name, His blood, and His Word. That is how you go against spiritual forces. Some Christians are afraid to testify, but your testimony is a praise to the Lord. When you speak out for Jesus, you come against the enemy.

Fasting is another weapon. You need to remember, however, that fasting does not change God. Fasting changes *you* and enables you to come against the devil with greater power. When you fast, it puts down the body and allows the spirit man to really be in charge. Fasting enables you to walk more in the spiritual realm than the natural.

Jesus fasted forty days before His encounter with Satan. And He told His disciples in Matthew 17:21 that a certain kind of demon **goeth not out but by prayer and fasting.** You can see from that verse that those two weapons, prayer and fasting, go together.

Fasting without spending extra time in prayer and fellowship with God will not be nearly as effective a weapon.

Jesus told His disciples to tarry in Jerusalem until the Holy Spirit came to endue them with power. (Acts 1:4,8.) In Ephesians 3:20, the Holy Spirit is called **the power that worketh in us.** The Holy Spirit was sent by God to help us show Jesus to the world and to give us the power to overcome the world and the devil.

If you turn the power of God loose in faith, it will put the devil on the run. The devil respects that power. On the Day of Pentecost, the Holy Spirit came upon the disciples and early Christians, and they were never the same.

He came to witness of Jesus and to work with the Body of Jesus to complete God's purpose on earth. It is not by our might nor power but by the power of the Holy Spirit that we can be more than conquerors. Paul constantly wrote that the signs and wonders and all things accomplished were done by the power of the Holy Spirit.

Now the God of hope fill you with all joy and peace in believing, that ye may abound in hope, through the power of the Holy Ghost.

Through mighty signs and wonders, by the *power* of the Spirit of God; so that from Jerusalem, and round about unto Illyricum, I have fully preached the gospel of Christ.

Romans 15:13,19

And there are many other references in the New Testament to the power of the Holy Spirit, so that it is easy to see that without Him, the saints' other weapons would not be nearly as effective.

Another weapon that most Christians today are not aware of is angels. We see them playing a part in Old Testament days, but somehow, most of us do not think angels still work with and for us. However, the Bible plainly tells us in Psalm 34:7 that angels camp around those who fear God and trust Him.

Angels protect us many times when we have no idea they are there. They are unseen weapons against demons. If you are out in the jungles of Africa to camp at night, you know to build a big fire and stay close to it. Lions, hyenas, wolves, and other animals will stay away from the fire. Angels are like a hedge of fire around us many times, and the demons stay away from them.

Do you trust and fear God? Then you should have no fear of the devil. You simply *know* that angels are camped around about you to handle what you cannot. However, you do not pray to angels. You do not worship angels. They are not divine, but created beings who have various functions for God. They are *His* servants and messengers.

You really should not even hold conversations with angels. You could be deceived by ''an angel of light,'' a demonic being. (2 Cor. 11:14.) An increasing number of Christians, however, have reported events involving angels in recent years.

I know of one man who was driving along a road, when he looked out to the side and saw a man dressed in white, riding a white horse.

He said to himself, ''What in the world is that?''

He was driving along at a good pace, perhaps fifty miles an hour, but the horse kept up with him. Then the horse galloped past him, and he thought it had left. But suddenly, the horse and rider were right in front of him. So he hit his brakes, and they disappeared.

When he got out of the car to look, he saw that the highway had caved in right in front of him. Apparently, there had not been time for the road crews to even put up signs. He would have been killed and the car totalled.

While he stood there leaning on the car hood, and looking at that hole in the road, he heard the Lord say, ''I'll guide you with mine eye.'' (Ps. 32:8.)

In Psalm 91:11,12, David wrote that the Lord will give His angels charge over us to keep us in all our ways. You may not even see the angels or be aware of their presence, but if you are a child of God, you have angels watching over you.

Consider Your Weapons

Just look at all the weapons God has given us to use against the enemy, in addition to the sword of the Spirit which is part of our armor. You do not even have to know all the weapons the enemy has to use against you. Whatever he has cannot prevail against you, if you *know* what you have and how to use them.

The Lord told us in Isaiah 54:17 what our heritage is and how strong we are in Him.

> **No weapon that is formed against thee shall prosper; and every tongue that shall rise against thee in judgment thou shalt condemn.** *This is the heritage* **of the servants of the Lord, and their righteousness is of me, saith the Lord.**

How can Christians let the devil run over them, much less backslide, when they have all these weapons? And I have not talked about the power of agreement or the power of being still in God yet.

Matthew 18:19 says that if two people on earth agree on anything within God's will, *it shall be done.* That is a pretty powerful weapon against anything the devil can bring against you as a married couple. When a husband and wife can agree, in prayer, then whatever they are praying for ought to come to pass quickly. A Christian husband and wife should be like one person.

Two chapters before this verse, Matthew wrote what Jesus said about "binding and loosing." That can be yet another weapon. The wisdom comes in knowing what needs binding and what needs loosing.

In Isaiah 30:15, the prophet wrote that strength can be found in quietness and confidence. Some people do not ever remain quiet. They must be master of the conversations. Everything must revolve around them. They know all the answers and want all the attention.

I have learned, however, that when you can be quiet and listen, you will know everything you already knew plus everything the people around you know. If you never listen, you never learn anything new. Some people are bored, however, if they are not the center of attention.

There is an old saying, "Still water runs deep." And that is very true. You would be surprised at the strength you gain simply by being quiet. Psalm 46:10 says, **Be still, and know that I am God.** You live in an "earthen vessel," so if you want God to be exalted in you, you must be still and know who He is.

There is great safety in the peace of the Lord. His peace, which comes from being still and quiet in Him, "insulates" you from the attacks of the enemy. He can still bring things against you, but you will not be moved by them. And if he cannot steal your joy and peace, the devil really cannot hurt you.

The last weapon I want to mention is *the anointing*. Isaiah 10:27 says that the anointing destroys the yoke of bondage. Therefore, the anointing of the Holy Spirit is a weapon against the enemy.

You may not need to know all of the enemy's tactics and weapons, but you do need to know enough about him to take him seriously.

4
The Devil Is Real

The devil is a real personality, a real supernatural being. Jesus dealt with him as a person, a spirit being. The devil is real, not just an evil principle or an abstract force of evil that opposes good. He literally exists and opposes the saints.

Satan is a "person," as you are a person. When the body dies, it will go back to the earth and decay. *You*, the person, will continue to live forever, either with God or in the regions of the damned. The body is not what makes you a person. Every human being is a person made up of spirit matter, the material of the supernatural realm. Bodies are simply what God provided for us to live and walk around in while we are in the natural realm.

The Godhead and all angelic beings are "persons," as are Satan, fallen angels, and demons. The devil is not a myth.

If Jesus dealt with Satan and demons as real, then so must we. However, you need to remember that the *Person* in you who deals with the devil is Jesus. You can shake your finger at the devil all you want, but your body will not move the devil.

After the devil's victorious encounter with Adam and Eve, the next place we learn much about him is in Job.

> **Now there was a day when the sons of God**
> (angels in this case) **came to present themselves before
> the Lord, and Satan came also among them.**
>
> **And the Lord said unto Satan, Whence comest
> thou? Then Satan answered the Lord, and said, From
> going to and fro in the earth, and from walking up
> and down in it.**
>
> **Job 1:6,7**

My thoughts and your thoughts are not God's
thoughts. I would have stopped the meeting and said,
"Get that rebellious cherub out of here! Didn't you get
enough whipping when you were thrown out of
Heaven? How dare you show your face around here
again?"

However, how He dealt with Satan is God's
business, not ours. All we are to know is that God is
just, and He does what is right. So He asked Satan
where he came from. After that came the entire
incident concerning Job, who loved God but was into
fear and self-righteousness. The end of that story was
victory for God and Job, because he repented and said,
for the first time, he really saw who God was. (Job
42:5.) Until then, he had been "good" through
religion, not through really knowing God.

The point is that in Job, the oldest book in the
Bible, as far as we know, Satan was written about as
a person. He traveled through the earth and
heavenlies; he attempted to defeat God's people; and,
he was a *real* enemy to Job. However, we also see that
strongholds in Job gave the enemy ground in which
to work.

Job feared God, but he did not trust Him.
Otherwise, he would not have been constantly going
behind his children and making sacrifices for fear they
had committed some sin that God would "get them"

for. (Job 1:5.) Does that sound like the idea some of us have of God? The wrong kind of fear of God makes ground for the enemy to keep you from really loving God.

God is not your enemy — the devil is, but you are not even to fear the devil. You are to trust in the armor and weapons God has given you, and put the devil under your feet. That is what Job eventually did, and then God could really bless him. (Job 42:12-17.)

Jesus said, in Luke 10:18, that He *saw* Satan fall as lightning from Heaven. Now, apparently, Satan's seat is in the second heavens, the realm between God's realm in the third heavens (2 Cor. 12:2), and the earth. In Ephesians 2:2, Paul called him "the prince of the power of the air." That means he literally still has the right to operate in that realm.

In Revelation 12:11,12, we are told of the final time of Satan's having any authority in the heavens or earth. At the time of the end, he will actually lose his place in the heavenlies and come to earth in great wrath, because he knows his time then will be very, very short.

The final judgment and disposal of Satan is foretold in Revelation 20:7,10, where John wrote that the devil would be bound a thousand years, then loosed for a time when he will gather all the nations against Jesus. Fire is to come down from Heaven and destroy all those human beings fighting with Satan, and then the devil will be cast into the lake of fire to remain forever.

His final end is to be no different from all of the human beings who have not accepted Jesus, therefore God is treating Satan as a person. His final prison will be the same as that of ungodly people. In other words, from Genesis to Revelation, Satan is spoken of as a real person.

The world calls Satan a myth, just as many of them think of God that way. Some Christians also seem to think the devil is simply a symbolic way of "personifying" evil. Other Christians operate in a delusion of optimism instead of faith.

They act as if the devil does not know "A from Z" and is a wimp. They believe that, because Jesus defeated him, he also was destroyed. Usually those same people blame God for what the devil is doing to them. All sickness, disease, or hard times is God "trying to teach me a lesson." No! Those things are the devil defeating them personally, when actually they have all power over all of his power.

Others have grabbed hold of a few scriptures, but have not trained themselves in using them. They do not really know warfare, but move out in presumption, not faith or spiritual ability.

Then the demons see them and say, "There's a juicy one. He is ripe for us. Let's get him!"

When his few verses quoted "by heart" and not from the spirit man do not run the devil off or quench his fiery darts, that Christian gets into self-pity and decides "all this faith stuff" does not work. It works, but he did not. Spiritual warfare is work. Fighting battles is work. It requires staying in prayer a lot, studying the Word a lot, and remaining vigilant against your foe.

Spiritual warfare means not being slack enough to let the devil even gain a toehold. Deal with the little things, and you can handle the big things. But if you let headaches and toe aches, scratches, and burns go by and think you can stand against cancer, you are badly mistaken. You must begin with small battles and develop the strength and knowledge to fight the big ones.

Satan Still Operates as God of This World

If the devil has observed human beings, generation in and generation out, for about six thousand years, as Bible scholars think, then he knows more about us than we know about ourselves. He knows much more about you than you know about him. He, in the persons of his demon troops, knows your ancestry and what weaknesses have been handed down to you.

You must wrap yourself in the armor of God, develop your weapons, and *know* (not just think) that the One in you is greater than the one in the world. You must *know* that God would not assign the Church of Jesus to put the devil underfoot if we could not do it.

In writing this way, I have no intention of shaking your faith. I simply know that all of us must know what we are going up against, as well as knowing our own position and strengths.

The apostles dealt with the devil as a real person, and the writers of the New Testament warned against a personal devil. (Eph. 6:10-18, 1 Thess. 2:18, 1 Pet. 5:8,9.)

Until the devil is put in his proper place, he still rules this world's systems as "god of this world (order)." (2 Cor. 4:4.) He does not own the planet. God reserved that right for Himself. (Ps. 50:12.) Nor does Satan legally have the right to dominion any longer. Jesus took that back from him and restored it to us. (Col. 2:14,15; 1 John 3:8; Rev. 5:10.)

In Genesis 1:26, *man* was given the dominion, the responsibility to rule over God's planet. However, as long as we — the Church — do not rise up and operate in authority, the devil still runs things in the world.

The devil is called by twenty-one different names or "titles" in Scripture. Some of them we have already mentioned. He is specifically called our enemy, the adversary, in Matthew 13:39 and 1 Peter 5:8. Some of the others are "father of lies" and "murderer" (John 8:44), "sower of discord" (Matt. 13:39), "tempter" (Matt. 4:1,2), "one who acts like a roaring lion" (1 Pet. 5:8), and Beelzebub (Matt. 12:24).

In 2 Corinthians 6:15, the devil is called Belial, which means "evil spirit." Names in ancient times were not just "labels," words by which to call things. Names had meanings, which told you something about the person, place, or thing. They were descriptions or definitions, not labels.

Satan did something or had some characteristic that caused him to be called by those twenty-one names. He is called "the adversary" because *he is.* That is not a label, but a definition. Apparently, his earliest name was *Lucifer,* which means "son of the morning, shining one, day star, son of the dawn."

The description of the purpose of his being created shows why this was his name. However, from the time he was cast out of the heavenlies taking a third of the angels — those who had rebelled against God — *Lucifer* is no longer his name.

In Ezekiel 28:12,13, God showed us through the prophet the beginnings of the being we know as our adversary. At that time, apparently Satan was the "king of Tyre," operating through the natural ruler

of that nation. And God sent him a message through
Ezekiel.

> **Son of man, take up a lamentation upon the king
> of Tyrus, and say unto him, Thus saith the Lord God;
> Thou sealest up the sum, full of wisdom, and perfect
> in beauty.**
>
> **Thou hast been in Eden the garden of God....**

You can see that the natural king, the human
being who was king of Tyre, could not possibly have
been in Eden, nor could he have fit the description that
follows. Lucifer is described as covered with all
precious jewels and having unimaginable musical
abilities. Then God said:

> **Thou art *the anointed cherub* that covereth; and
> I have set thee so: thou wast upon the holy mountain
> of God; thou hast walked up and down in the midst
> of the stones of fire.**
>
> **Thou wast perfect in thy ways from the day that
> thou wast created, till iniquity was found in thee.**
>
> **Ezekiel 28:14,15**

God then listed why the devil rebelled (vanity over
his beauty, pride, and self-will), and what his end will
be. That is to be exposed as a worm and failure before
all the people of earth, to be brought to ashes in the
sight of all (Ez. 28:17-19), which is the judgment
foretold in Revelation 20:10.

People say to me, "Don't talk about the devil. You
will just magnify him. Talk about Jesus."

Yes, we need to talk about Jesus, and part of
talking about Jesus is talking about the things He said
about our adversary and how we must deal with him.
To talk only about Jesus and neglect Jesus' words about
the devil is to say:

"You already are a champion. You do not need
to train. You do not need to know how to fight. You
are not in a battle."

If Christians are not involved in warfare, why did Paul refer to us as "soldiers"? Why did he say we need armor and weapons? Why did he refer to the Christian walk as "a fight"?

When you are not trained in spiritual warfare, the enemy will "pin your ears back." If you were planning to become a boxer or a wrestler, you would train to deal with the kind of opponent you have — just as a soldier in the armed services is trained to fight his opposite numbers in whatever nation the particular enemy is in at the time.

In boxing, you have the slugger who has no style but just keeps doggedly slugging away until he or his opponent is knocked out. Then you have the "pretty" boxer whom everyone likes to watch, the one who can put on a good show, like Muhammad Ali. You have the kind of boxer who has no long-distance stamina, so he has trained to give you a knock-out punch early on in the match. Also, you have the "in-fighter," the one who gets you in a clench and fights until you are out of wind.

Boxers in training practice on punching bags, and they "shadow box," going through all of the motions of feinting, punching, and evading punches but with an imaginary opponent. Christians never need to shadow-box. Paul said he did not fight that way, "as one who beats at the air." (1 Cor. 9:26.)

Because of the strength of the flesh and the potential it has for the devil to use it against you, Paul said he treated his body as an opponent. He worked to keep it under subjection. That was a form of spiritual warfare — preventive warfare to remove a "hole" through which his real opponent might attack.

You should know your opponent. A champion fighter does not rest on his laurels and make no effort to find out what his next opponent is like. He does not stop training unless he is retired or has lost heart in the fight and does not care whether or not he wins.

Even Christians who know they are soldiers and who engage in spiritual warfare sometimes fall into the trap of thinking there is only one way to fight. If "binding and loosing" have worked before, they do not familiarize themselves with the other weapons God has provided. However, demons do not all fight alike, and the same weapons will not work in each case.

Actually, every fight is different, because there are different kinds of spirits coming against you. You cannot always simply quote the Word, "It is written." Jesus did that in one instance, but then He "cast out" demons, fought spirits of infirmity in different ways, even to spitting in blind eyes.

The sons of Sceva, about whom Luke wrote in the book of Acts, made the mistake of underestimating the demons. They moved in presumption, not a true knowledge of Jesus. And the demons in the possessed man with whom they were dealing jumped out of him and onto them, tore off their clothes, and sent them running down the street naked and bleeding. The demons whipped their shoes off. (Acts 19:14-18.)

The demons know when you have it and when you do not. The demons said about Sceva's sons that they knew Jesus and they knew Paul, but who were these guys? Do the demons know you? They certainly know when you qualify as a fighter!

You cannot quote the Word and be victorious when there is no death of self, no consecration, and no commitment in your life. I do not care how much Bible you know or how much you quote scriptures, the devil knows who you are. He *knows* those Christians who truly are God's.

Do you know who *he* is? The medieval Church did us a disservice by illustrating the devil with horns, hooves, and a tail. They made a "myth" out of him by showing him with a pitchfork presiding over hell, the lake of fire. He is not presiding over the lake of fire, and he will not be presiding over it. He will be burning in it along with everyone else who has been cast there because of their choices against Jesus.

So you need to know your adversary is real and, until he is put underfoot forever, he rules over most of the systems of the world — political, educational, economic, cultural, and even in some cases, religious systems.

Satan is the chief devil, the original source of evil in the universe, the only prince of devils. However, there are many fallen angels and many, many demons.

Demons Also Are Real

Demons are disembodied spirits that cannot operate in the material world to their fullest, except through the bodies of men or animals. They oppress, obsess, and possess. They also tend to operate in groups. One gets into a body somewhere and calls to all his friends that he has found a good place.

The man from whom Jesus cast out a "legion" of demons contained from three thousand to six thousand of them. None of those were *the* devil. The Bible talks about Jesus casting out "unclean" spirits. *All of them are unclean.* There is nothing clean about any demonic spirit.

Jesus said that when an unclean spirit goes out of a person, it walks to and fro through dry places looking for another "house." (Matt. 12:43.) After a certain period of time, the demon goes back to his old house to see if he can get back inside. If the house has been cleaned and not filled with the Holy Spirit, it is clean but empty.

That demon says, "All you did was clean and decorate your house for me. Come on, brothers, here is a good place to live," and he calls seven others in *more wicked than himself.* Therefore, the last state of the person is worse than the first, Jesus said. (Matt. 12:44,45.)

That person really is possessed. There is a difference in demonic control, demonic influence, and demonic possession. The Bible says that Jesus went about doing good, "healing all that were oppressed." He did not "heal" those that were possessed. With those people, he "cast out" demons.

Here are some things about demons that show you they are real, and they have different personalities and different assignments:

*Demons can be intelligent and wise, or they can be fairly dumb — just like people. The demon in the woman who followed Paul in Acts 16:16-18 brought her masters much gain through telling the future.

*Demons are not angels. In Acts 23:8,9, a distinction is made between "spirits" (demons) and "angels."

*Demons have knowledge of people. (Acts 19:15, Matt. 8:29.)

*Demons believe in God. (James 2:19.) There is no way they cannot believe there is a God. They live in the supernatural realm where they have more literal awareness of the existence of God than we do. They know for certain all of the things in the Bible that we must believe on faith.

*Demons have feelings. (Mark 5:7,8; Acts 8:7.)

*Demons can have "fellowship" with people. (1 Cor. 10:20,21.)

*Demons can teach doctrines, false interpretations or twisted ways of understanding God's Word. (1 Tim. 4:1.)

*Demons can be powerful, depending on what kind they are. (Mark 5:1-18.)

*Demons are evil. (1 Sam. 18:9,10.)

*Demons *can* be cast out — not asked to leave, but thrown out. (Matt. 10:17.) This last characteristic may be the most important one to Christians learning about spiritual warfare. No matter how powerful they are, you have the power and the authority (through the Holy Spirit and the name of Jesus) to cast them out.

These things should not be hard to believe. After you die, you will be able to think. You will have feelings. Why would we believe demons, fallen angels, or the devil do not? The Bible says that, in hell, there will be wailing and gnashing of teeth because of the torment of the flames. (Matt. 13:42,50.) That does not mean only people will be undergoing the awful conditions of the eternal prison of the wicked. All spirit beings in there will be undergoing the same conditions.

Apparently, some very powerful spirits will be released in the last days. (Rev. 16:13,14.) They will be allowed to deal with nations, not individuals. I believe we are moving into the time when the Church must deal with more powerful spirits. That is why God wants His people trained and ready.

America's rebellious years of the Sixties brought much more powerful demons into this country, and the more society has yielded to them, the more have poured into the United States.

Pastors and evangelists who minister to the needs of people must begin to understand they will be dealing with heavier spirits. Some of those demons will jump off on the ministers and their helpers, if they are not prayed up and walking in sanctification.

In the next chapter, I want to talk more about the powers of darkness, not to bring any sort of fear. Fear of man or demons is not of God. (2 Tim. 1:7.) I want Christians to know the truth. I want them to understand what is going on in the world and what we are facing as the army of the Lord.

5

The Powers of Darkness

The powers of darkness really got a hold on this country when all of the rebellion began against the "establishment." Rebellion against the flag, the government, parents, the law, morality, and of course, the Church. The rebellious generation was born during World War II, when most fathers were off at war and mothers began to be "liberated."

That "baby boomer" generation did not learn authority as older generations had. They were not taught respect for Church, family, and law and order. Many of them grew up with parents absent or too busy to give them proper love and attention. Today, that situation is a common condition in society. Then, it was just beginning.

The devil hates marriage as God designed it, and he hates a good family life. So the powers of darkness infiltrated the "empty" spaces left by absent fathers and busy mothers. Any area you leave empty in your life, or in our church and national life, is fair game for the powers of darkness.

The young people expressed their resentment and hatred in "protests." They stopped taking baths and wearing decent, clean clothes. They began to literally "look like the devil." They began to go around with long hair and dirty clothes.

Demons had a field day with that generation. Young people experimented with drugs, opened their minds to demons of oppression, darkness, and even suicide. Violence has become a way of life today. By the Eighties, it seems many people were "obsessed" with blood, violent crimes, and demonic concepts.

One thing led to another. Marijuana turned into cocaine, then into heroin, and now into much more dangerous drugs. The built-in desire for the supernatural, which God intended to turn man toward Him, became perverted into a desire for the wrong kind of supernatural experience.

LSD brought "mind trips," talk of "expanded consciousness," and "out-of-body" experiences. All of those things are simply the opening up of the mind and spirit to demons. The spirits of sexual perversion and sadism were loosed into this country. Well-known musicians and entertainment figures brought in demons of Eastern mysticism.

People today get thrills out of seeing someone being hurt. Most of them still indulge this dark, satanic impulse vicariously through movies, television, and so forth. However, if it continues, there is no way you will not begin to see it more and more in real life.

Today, people seem obsessed with ugliness — E.T., the "Beast" on the television program by that name, and "heroes" such as the young man who had scissors for hands. Somehow, ugliness and darkness are being "preached" into our society as "good," and Christianity is being portrayed as "evil."

That is what Paul wrote happened to mankind before the flood. What he said they did has been a pattern down through the centuries, because when Noah's descendants began to multiply, they followed the same spiritual route, enticed by the powers of darkness.

> **Professing themselves to be wise, they became fools,**
>
> **And changed the glory of the uncorruptible God into an image made like to corruptible man, and to birds, and fourfooted beasts, and creeping things.**
>
> **Wherefore God also gave them up to uncleanness through the lusts of their own hearts, to dishonour their own bodies between themselves:**
>
> **Who changed the truth of God into a lie, and worshipped and served the creature more than the Creator, who is blessed for ever.**
>
> **Romans 1:22-25**

In our time, we have seen this happen. We have seen those people professing to be wise turn the truth of God into a lie. We have seen darkness creep more and more over this country. Verse 28 says that, because they did not like to keep God in their knowledge, He gave them over to "reprobate minds."

People who dishonour their own bodies, who change the truth of God into a lie, become open prey for the powers of darkness. How can we defend ourselves, much less help those pitiful, deluded people, if we do not recognize the powers of darkness as real? How can we help, if we do not know how to fight the real sources of all of this ugliness, hatred, and violence?

We *must* learn who the enemy is. When God moved among that rebellious generation in what became known as "the Jesus movement," many churches mistakenly thought their enemy was the people who had been "hippies." Many Christian churches refused to allow them into their services, even after they were born again. Certainly, they would not have attempted to get them delivered and free from darkness!

Those Christians who helped free that generation are in the minority. Do we want to be a minority like that in the Nineties? Or do we want to stand up and be counted in the service of the Lord Jesus Christ? Do we want to "do the works of Jesus?" Then we need to learn how to cast out demons, heal the oppressed, and resist the devil. That was a large part of Jesus' ministry.

Sometimes, *oppressed* people get delivered when they get saved. Sometimes they are "healed" during special prayer or through intensive prayers of their own. Possessed people, however, must have the demon or demons involved cast out of them. *To be oppressed* means "to be overloaded, to having something that wears heavily on mind, spirit, or body, to be trampled under, to be pressed against."

Paul said:

> We are troubled on every side, yet not distressed; we are perplexed, but not in despair;
>
> Persecuted, but not forsaken; cast down, but not destroyed.
>
> 2 Corinthians 4:8,9

Oppression, Obsession, and Possession

Obviously, being oppressed does not mean you are not saved, and it does not mean the devil has the upper hand. It simply means that temporarily you have been "overloaded." However, if you are oppressed, it is of the devil. If oppression was of God, why would He have sent Jesus to heal it?

Demonic *obsession* means having an irresistible urge or desire, a compulsion, to perform certain acts, think certain thoughts, or indulge in certain substances. Any addiction, compulsion, or obsession involves demons. If you have a "tendency" toward certain things, or are tempted by certain things, but you can take authority over your actions, then you are dealing with strongholds in your own mind, not demonic influence. However, if you let those thoughts and imaginations go on, as we discussed earlier, you more than likely will come under demonic control. Those thoughts and desires then develop into obsessions, compulsions, or addictions.

When you are "down," I do not care how "up" your body is, you are oppressed. You are dejected, sad, gloomy, and depressed. The epidemic of depression that has been sweeping this country is the end result of *oppression*. When you move into acute or chronic "depression," oppression has developed into demonic control or influence.

If you feel depressed or oppressed over anything, learn to recognize that feeling as the ground for, or the beginning of, an onslaught of the enemy. Fight it right then! Begin to pray or sing in the Spirit and worship God. His joy will rise up and cleanse you of those negative feelings, if you stay at it.

Losing your job is a signal to praise and worship God, because He is your Father. You know from His Word that He will take care of you and provide another as good or better. Begin to look on things like that as opportunities, not defeats. The devil cannot defeat you, if you do not let him. Half of his defeat is in oppressing your mind or emotions. Then your will is handicapped in its agreement with the Holy Spirit.

Depression can cause you to backslide, to commit spiritual suicide. It can cause you to commit physical suicide. Do not let it have free reign in your life, or you are already beaten by the devil. If nothing else, depression will make openings for sicknesses to come on you.

You cannot deal with it by sitting and whining, "Lord, help me out of this."

You must get up and physically move out of the place where you are. Get out of bed, get out of the house, get out into the sunshine. Get into the car and go for a drive. Take a shower or wash the car. Go visiting. Go downtown and window shop. Do something to break up the hypnotic influence some demon is exerting over you.

Best of all, move out and find something to do for someone else. Put down your own feelings to reach out and meet someone else's need. As the body moves in action, the mind will begin to throw off the negative thoughts, and those thoughts will disappear.

In this case, your weapon is action *in faith* that negative thoughts cannot stay in the presence of positive actions. Being a "Good Samaritan" will also defeat the devil, if those deeds are done out of the righteousness of the heart and not out of religion or for men's approval.

I will not let demons get me into despair. God did not bring me this far to leave me. And He does not have to tell me something every minute for me to believe it. My past knowledge of His Word and His actions are enough for me to believe Him in the future.

There are demons of *recession*. That means to fall away from an activity during a period when such activity should be increased. When you should be moving forward, you are moving backward. You are regressing, which is all *recession* is. When you ought to be going forward, the devil has you backing up.

The final state of someone who has yielded to oppression, recession, and depression is *possession*. A possessed person cannot be a Christian, because the Holy Spirit and a demon cannot reside in the same house. The Holy Spirit resides in your spirit man, and oppression or influence affects the soul and body. Possession means the devil has control of *the real you*. Therefore, the Holy Spirit cannot have total authority.

If you get hit with a virus, that does not mean you are not born again. If you come under an attack of oppression or even depression, it does not mean you are not born again. However, if the devil is controlling your every thought and act, then you really *are not* born again.

Demons are disembodied spirits looking for a home. If they cannot find a person, they will possess animals. I believe it was old-time Evangelist Charles Finney who would get off a train to proceed to the place where he was to hold a revival, and ask the person who met him with horse and carriage — or horses and buckboard — if the animals were tame.

He walked so close to the Lord that all he had to do was walk by a place of business or a tavern, and people would fall under conviction. He was totally sold out to the Lord. But he had some experiences where he would get off the train and get into a conveyance of some kind, only to have the horses stand up on their hind legs at the same time, come down on all fours, and start running.

The demons assigned to try and stop his meetings had possessed those horses and were trying to kill him.

I have had experiences where demons even inhabited articles of witchcraft and sorcery that had been given up when someone was saved. When I wanted to take some of those things home from an overseas meeting once to show my people the devil's implements, I became nauseated as I handled them.

I did not say a word out loud, but began to quietly tell those demons they were liars. I resisted the sickness, and it went away.

Another time I was preaching about demons, and I began to hear them crying. I heard this in the spirit, not out loud.

I said to the people, "There are demons in this place, and I can hear them crying."

A woman suddenly jumped up from the back and ran toward the front. The demon in her tried to bite my hand, but we prayed and cast it out. God delivered her.

The same thing happened with a man sitting in the back. Any time you speak on demons, demonology, the powers of darkness, or witchcraft and sorcery, any demons present will get stirred up. Those can be dealt with in the service, if the person on whom they stay will allow it.

Demons will try to kill you outright — through sickness and disease, through accidents, or through violence from animals or other people. If they are not able to kill you, because of your place in God or because of someone else's prayers over you, they will try to oppress you mentally and emotionally. Or they will attack your ministry in an attempt to kill it.

Why do you think that viper crawled out of the wood on the island of Melita and bit Paul? He was not the only one helping build that fire. It bit him because he was a chosen vessel. The devil knew that it was through Paul all two hundred and seventy-six people on board that wrecked ship had been saved. (Acts 27; 28:1-5.)

The devil knew how many souls had been saved through Paul, and how many more down through the centuries would owe their salvation, sanctification, or ministry to the writings of the Apostle Paul. He had not been able to stop him so far, although demons certainly had tried. But now a demon saw a chance to get him.

But what happened? Even a deadly viper's bite could not kill Paul. Why? He had learned spiritual warfare. He knew demons were real, but he knew how to overcome — through the blood of Jesus and the authority of His name. He had walked in the armor of God so long that he knew there was no danger until his work for God was finished. And he already had been told by God that he must testify of Him in Rome as he had in Jerusalem before the Sanhedrin. (Acts 23:11.)

The devil had it in for Paul, just as he had for Jesus, and will have for us — if we are doing something to hurt him. According to Church history, the devil finally got Paul put to death. But when that occurred, Paul had "finished his course." He had completed the purpose God had for him, and the devil only helped Paul on his way to the Father.

Demons of Subtlety
Few Christians will have to deal with those very powerful demons, the ones that have been given a

"contract" on someone. All of us should be alert, however, for the more subtle ones. Sometimes demons are waiting for you when you wake up in the morning. You must learn to resist the devil as soon as you open your eyes. There are others that will attack you in your sleep. And sometimes people come to visit your home and leave a demon spirit.

If you suddenly get up one morning and feel differently about your spouse, resist a demon. If someone visits, and after they leave, your house is full of strife and contention, cast that spirit that was left out of the house.

Demons that are powerful, yet subtle, are the ones that "bewitch" people in modern society. Most Christians know enough to stay away from witchcraft or "voodoo," such as is very prevalent in Haiti, for example. However, many of them fall under the spell of seemingly harmless musicians or television programs.

Bewitched means "to be driven out of your senses, your right mind." When groups like the Beatles began to come into this country as part of the years of rebellion, many thousands — perhaps millions — of teenagers became bewitched.

Singers, such as Elvis Presley, operated under what amounted to a false anointing. When people are out of their senses enough to faint or try to tear the clothes off an entertainer, they are *bewitched*. A spell had been cast over them by the powers of darkness. They were "charmed" out of their normal, proper way of acting.

Another subtle demon is "a spirit of control." Parents who control their grown children as if they were still small and under authority are operating under a spirit. Wives, or husbands, who manipulate their spouses into doing what they want are operating under a demon of control.

Anyone who uses sex, love (emotional satisfaction and needs), or money to bend other people to his, or her, will is operating under a "spirit of control." We tend to think a "spirit of Jezebel" only affects women, but it can also attach itself to men.

Another weapon of the enemy that can be very subtle or very obvious is *fear*. A government, such as the Soviet Union used to be, operates under a powerful and very obvious "ruler of the darkness of this world." (Eph. 6:12.)

Even some church leaders control their congregations through a spirit of fear. They even misuse the "gifts of the Spirit" to control people. Of course, they are not operating in a real, true gift, but a counterfeit, a false tongue or prophecy.

"The Lord told me that if you walk out that door without giving me (money, or whatever), you will get cancer. You will die in six weeks, if you do not obey me."

That is not of God! That is nothing but a spirit of witchcraft, whether it operates through bewitchment that seems fun and good or through a spirit of fear.

Other related spirits are occultism, divination, sorcery, superstition, and familiar spirits.

To one with knowledge of the Word of God, these powers of darkness are obvious. However, to the world that believes the devil *and* God are myths, they are subtle entrapments. All of them operate through bewitchment.

Occultism involves anything of **the depths of Satan** ("the secret things" — Rev. 2:24). That is what the word *occult* means — something secret or hidden. Modern *spiritism* or *spiritualism* surfaced in the mid-1800s in New York State, when a couple of women, the Fox sisters, began to communicate with demons, and later, with "spirits of the dead."

The craze for the unorthodox and forbidden experimentation with the supernatural soon spread across Europe as well. Even a church (denomination) of spiritualism was established, which still has branches in many places. Demons, under the guise of the spirits of the dead, are invited into the services and actually give utterances that counterfeit the gifts of the Spirit.

Those involved have been bewitched into believing a lie as truth. If you are not aware of the difference, you can go into those churches and be fooled. They sing, read the Bible, pray, speak in "tongues" sometimes, and act like "holiness" folks.

Spiritism believes there is no separation of people after death, and the New Age movement has adopted this doctrine into its beliefs. Most believe there is a hereafter, but they believe everyone goes to a beautiful place called "Summerland." This goes along with the doctrine of reincarnation, which comes from Eastern religions.

After a certain resting period as a spirit, they believe you come back and are "born again" (Satan's counterfeit of conversion) into another body, whose condition and fate depend on what you deserve. This is simply another variation of "works" instead of grace. You "earn" what you get. You deserve the kind of life you have, because you have developed it in past lives.

Many people have been bewitched in recent years into believing this "doctrine of man."

These "spirits of the dead," which really are what the Bible calls "familiar spirits," manifest usually through a person who has given over control of his, or her, mind to a demon. This familiar spirit speaks through this person and pretends to be a loved one of someone present, or a famous person of the past who has died.

Those demons are "knowledgeable." They either actually oppressed or influenced those dead persons, so they know all about their lives and personalities, or they have access to that information through another demon.

The case of Saul and the witch of Endor is an example of familiar spirits. (1 Sam. 28:7-19.) The prophet Samuel had died (1 Sam. 25:1), and Saul could get no counsel from anyone. God already had rejected him, pronounced judgment, and anointed another king (David) to serve after Saul's death. So Saul sought information from a familiar spirit.

Israel had been told not to allow a witch to live (Ex. 22:18), yet the king of Israel invoked the powers of darkness. In Deuteronomy 18:10, Moses had written an even stronger decree against witches, sorcerers, and "diviners of times." However, Saul's men knew right away where someone like that was still operating in Israel!

I do not believe it was really Samuel who came forth from the supernatural to speak to Saul, because God would not answer him by dream, vision, or prophet who was alive. (1 Sam. 28:6.) Why would God then allow the spirit of the prophet to come forth? God had departed from Saul and taken the Holy Spirit from him.

Some people believe the witch was a fake, that she was surprised a spirit manifested. Whatever the case, Saul believed it was Samuel, and he believed what the apparition told him: God has taken the kingdom out of your hand and given it to David. Because of you, Israel will be delivered into the hand of the Philistines, and furthermore, tomorrow you and your sons will be with me.

Saul certainly did not hear any good news, and what the spirit said came true. Some such words are self-fulfilling. For example, if Saul and his sons believed that really was Samuel, perhaps they did not fight as hard. Or perhaps the demons heard what Samuel had prophesied to Saul years before over the incident with the Amalekites (1 Sam. 15:17-26), and they knew it was time for those words to be fulfilled.

You can have faith in negative things as well as positive and have them come to pass. The use of pendulums or a ouiji board is a type of spiritism, using objects as mediums instead of people.

Witchcraft also involves powers of darkness that are more obvious, such as black magic, the black arts, sorcery, and fortune telling (palm reading, tea-leaf reading, tarot cards, and so forth). These types of fortune telling actually are what is called *divination*. They counterfeit words of wisdom and knowledge, also prophecy.

Soothsaying is the devil's form of prophecy. As he is not all-knowing, more often than not these words are false. Or, if they do come true, it is because someone put faith in them, which allowed a demon to bring the word to pass in that person's life.

Yet another prevalent power of darkness since the Sixties has been astrology. During the decade of rebellion, occultism of all kinds seemed to explode into this country. Astrology is one many Christians have fallen into, thinking it is a harmless game of some sort. There have been Christians, even ministers, who set out to learn all about astrology in order to teach against it, but instead, they became "infected" with the virus of sorcery and succumbed to its influence.

More often, however, Christians become involved through curiosity. It never pays to be curious about the devil's territory, whether it is alcohol, drugs, witchcraft, or astrology. If Christians knew their Bibles as well as some of them know the zodiac, the devil would not be able to steal as many souls from the Church.

Some people read their horoscope in the newspaper more religiously each day than they do the Bible! All of those things are of the devil. People can cause them to come to pass, however, through negative faith.

You may think superstitions are harmless, just as many people do astrology. They include everything from carrying a "lucky charm" or "a lucky object" of some kind to believing that, because your daddy died at a certain age, you will. Believe those things long enough, and some power of darkness will see that it comes to pass.

The wave of occultism that has swept this country also uses oils, incense, and candles very heavily. Those are objects the powers of darkness operate through, along with certain "spells," rituals, and incantations.

Saints, please do not be "seat-warmer Christians." Get in God, and let the Holy Spirit have

His way in you, so that you may be able to survive such times as these. The powers of darkness are very real. Go back to the Word, and read the Great Commission again. That is a prophecy for *you* as well as a commandment.

> **And these signs shall follow them that believe; In my name shall they cast out devils; they shall speak with new tongues;**
>
> **They shall take up serpents; and if they drink any deadly thing, it shall not hurt them; they shall lay hands on the sick, and they shall recover.**
>
> **Mark 16:17,18**

You have been deputized to follow in the footsteps and do the works of your "Chief," the Lord Jesus Christ. We must be up and about the Master's business.

6
Power Over the Enemy

We should thank God that we are Jesus' deputies, and we ought to remember that a deputy does not tell the high sheriff he does not want to go on duty! God does not *make* you a deputy. You "volunteer" when you become born again. He does not "draft" you into the army or into service as a deputy. It goes with the territory.

The story in Luke 10 of Jesus deputizing seventy disciples never ceases to amaze me. He sent them out to minister, telling them the harvest was great and laborers were few. (Luke 10:1-16.) He told them not only to be "advance men" for him (v. 1), but to "heal the sick."

This incident happened *before* the Holy Spirit came on the Day of Pentecost. The seventy were not filled with the Spirit, yet Jesus deputized them as much as He did all Christians later when He spoke forth the "Great Commission."

Luke wrote that, after a period of time, the seventy "returned with joy." (v. 17.) Their joy was because they had found that devils were subject to them by the name of Jesus. Then Jesus answered them this way:

> **And he said unto them, I beheld Satan as lightning fall from heaven.**

> Behold, I give unto you power to tread on
> serpents and scorpions, and over *all the power* of the
> enemy: and nothing shall by any means hurt you.
>
> Notwithstanding in this rejoice not, that the
> spirits are subject unto you; but rather rejoice, because
> your names are written in heaven.
>
> Luke 10:18-20

This was even before the death, burial, and
resurrection of Jesus! Even more than demons being
subject to them, Jesus told them to rejoice over their
names being written in Heaven.

They had power from Him before they left. They
were told to heal the sick. But when they returned,
He increased their power, giving them the ability to
tread on serpents and scorpions and *all the power* of
the enemy.

He was saying, "You thought you had power
before you left on this evangelistic trip. But I saw Satan
fall like lightning. I knew you were being used by the
Father, because I saw Satan's defeat. Now, you have
power over his power."

We must understand, from the context, that Jesus
was talking about demons when He said "serpents and
scorpions." *Tread* means "to step on." Jesus was
telling them then that the least in the Kingdom has all
power over the enemy.

The seventy went out, came back, and received
more power — but you never hear of them again. I
wonder what happened to them?

Before this — some scholars say about a year
before — Jesus had sent the twelve out to the "lost
sheep" of Israel, giving them the same kind of power:

> And when he had called unto him his twelve
> disciples, he gave them power against unclean spirits,
> to cast them out, and to heal all manner of sickness
> and all manner of disease.

These twelve Jesus sent forth, and commanded them, saying, ...

. . . The kingdom of heaven is at hand.

Heal the sick, cleanse the lepers, raise the dead, cast out devils: freely ye have received, freely give.
Matthew 10:1,5,7,8

In many of our churches, we are teaching and preaching about the power of God, the name of Jesus, and the authority of the believer — yet we are doing little treading on "serpents and scorpions." There is a difference between authority and power — a vast difference, but neither will do us any good, if we do not use them.

Authority means "the right to give orders, official approval, commands."

Power is the force or the ability to enforce authority. Our authority lies in the name of Jesus, based on His work at Calvary that restored dominion to God's people. Our power comes from the Holy Spirit, who is the Enforcer of our authority.

The Difference Between Authority and Power

A policeman does not have to be a huge guy to walk in the authority of the law. However, sometimes he has to have back up in the form of other policemen or weapons in order to *enforce* his authority. He must have the *power* of the local, state, or national government behind him when he deals with hard cases.

He can be so small that, when you look at his back, the pockets meet where the pants had to be taken in to fit him. But no matter his size, he does not have to use his gun, his billy club, or yell in order to have the authority to make an arrest. When he stops a car and asks to see your driver's license, most of the time, he gets no argument at all. We all know his authority.

There are some demons like that. The seventy apparently ran into those kinds of demons. They recognized the authority Jesus had given those men. Demons knew the seventy were deputies of the Son of God, a Kingdom posse.

Later, some of the twelve disciples ran into some demons that were not so easy to bring under authority. Those cases required the power of the Holy Spirit that only is available through prayer and fasting. (Matt. 17:21.)

Then there are some "strong men" who require the power of an entire posse to take them under arrest. We need to know how to move forward as an army, not just platoons, regiments, battalions, and so forth. In times to come, I believe there will be "principalities, powers, rulers of the darkness of this world, and spiritual wickedness in high places" (Eph. 6:12) that will require the declaring of Kingdom "martial law."

A large portion of the army, or the posse, will have to be called into duty to deal with them, if the Church is to survive. Jesus said the gates of hell would not prevail against His Church. (Matt. 16:18) Like the early Christians, we may have to prove that.

We cannot work together as a King's posse with spirits of indifference, wrong attitudes at one another, jealousy and envy, or judging and holding grudges. Those attitudes are dividing our forces even now. When the enemy can keep us divided, we will be overrun although we have all the authority we need. Division of our forces stops our power from being effective.

I have noticed that, in times of rebellion against their authority, most policemen talk real nice and quiet until they see those flashing blue back-up lights coming.

I heard one say once, "I'm not crazy! I'm waiting. When I see two of those great big Irish cops coming in here, that's when I back up behind them. I'll back them up, but I have better sense than to go in by myself."

There is a time to call for reinforcements. If you run into a demonic situation where you know the authority is there but the power is not flowing through you like it ought, call for back up. Get in unity with your pastor or other Christians, and begin to fast and pray to deal with that thing.

Then make up your mind that you are going to exercise in order not to be caught short another time. Find out where your weak areas are — body, mind, or spirit; carnal desires and urges, attitudes and doubt or disbelief, lack of faith or prayer — wherever it is, take care of it.

In any case, you had better stay behind Jesus. He is the big power, the only authority and power that demons recognize. If you want to be an effective member of this endtime army, decide right now to not stop at having authority. Decide to go on to the fullness of walking in the power.

When a posse is deputized, all of them cannot shoot straight. Some of them might hardly be able to stay on a horse. Some of them end up running behind. However, all have been deputized, and if you hang around power long enough, some of it will rub off on you.

I am not being critical or judging, but the fact remains that many Christians have been deputized but do not have the power to deliver victory. A policeman's .44 Magnum is his "equalizer." No matter his size compared to that of the one he is arresting, that gun equalizes the situation.

The sword of the Spirit is your equalizer. The power of the Holy Spirit is your back up. The name of Jesus is your authority, and His blood is what deputized you. You are in the service of the Lord God Almighty, whether you realize it or not. Your choice is only whether to be a good soldier, a good servant, a good deputy — or a mediocre one.

In times to come, you are going to be "picked on" by demonic bullies, no matter what you do, so you are going to have to learn to agonize in prayer and use all the other weapons available to you. In order to free addicts and those bound by homosexuality or infirmities — even AIDS — God must have a people who are shouldering the burden and willing to do what is necessary to give Him the total victory.

Of course, Jesus could have finished off the devil at the cross. As well as defeating him, Jesus could have destroyed him. He could have been put in the lake of fire then. However, God's purpose for the earth and for man from the beginning of creation was to have man take dominion over the earth.

Taking dominion means running the enemies out of your territory. God's purposes always will be fulfilled. He is never defeated, although His purposes can be hindered by us for a time. That is because He chose to give us the right to make choices, then made a way for us to repent when we make the wrong ones. However, He always has His will and His way. If we want Jesus to come back soon, the Church must stand up and move into fulfilling her purpose.

This "gospel of the Kingdom" must be preached to the whole world. Then the end will come. (Matt. 24:14.) To preach God's purpose and plans, we must run out the enemy before us as Israel did when they took the Promised Land under Joshua.

You will notice that God gave them the land, and they fought according to His plans and in His might. However, they had to fight. They had a part in the victory. God could have cleaned out the land for them, but His will was for them to do what they could. Things that come to you too easily are very seldom valued, and God knows that about us.

What Is the Role of a Deputy?

A *deputy* is an assistant employed to act as a substitute in the absence of his superior. The Bible refers to that role as "a steward," one who has total responsibility to look after and increase His Master's holdings and authority to act in the Master's name.

Jesus is saying to us, "You are My deputies. I gave you something the Seventy did not have. They took the little I gave them and used it to the maximum. I had to give them some more. You are born again, filled with the Spirit, speaking in tongues, and have all power over the enemy — and what are you doing?

"Demons are romping over you and raging in your homes, your bodies, and your jobs, even in your churches. It is too late in the day to sit in church looking nice. The devil is not paying any attention to you, and you are not doing My works."

Rise up! We *must* begin to exercise our spiritual authority and walk in the power of the Holy Spirit.

Otherwise, we are like the unprofitable servant. (Matt. 25:14-30.) We must begin to act like deputies of the most powerful Being in the universe, the One Who owns everything. We must begin to act like the Lord's "posse" on earth, and we must begin to round up the "bad guys." It does our Master no credit to have the world see the bad guys beat up on us.

God is looking for a posse that will live up to their covenant with Him, their responsibility to uphold His commands.

The problem is that we like to exercise natural power, as we saw earlier that Peter did. We like to have natural titles and offices and to have secular authority, even authority in the church.

We throw our weight around, act like petty tyrants on the job, in our homes, and in our churches, and think we are "ruling and reigning." All the time, the devil is urging us on, "Yeah! Yeah! That's the way to do it," and the Holy Spirit is grieved.

All of the time, we cannot even exercise enough spiritual authority to get a headache off of someone. Anyone who looks around at society today with half an eye can tell these are the days when we must live in a realm of power over the devil if we are going to make it.

Spiritual exercise operates on the same principle as natural exercise to build up the body. You begin with something small that you can lift, then you progress to heavier and heavier weights. You do not have to begin by "pumping" two hundred and fifty pounds. Start with a few minutes each morning, lifting "twenty-five pounds."

When you do that, your lungs will begin to develop and the blood will flow better through your circulatory system. You will be surprised how active you feel very quickly.

Christians who do no spiritual "exercise" at home but rely on praying a little, singing a little, and praising God a little at church once a week have flabby spiritual muscles. Begin exercising spiritually at home.

Stop looking for sensationalism, the latest "fad" in conference circles. Stop running around following someone who has a "deep" ministry. You are still in the same place you were in five years ago. Those ministers have been fasting, praying, and seeking God until He gave them something. Go after your own things from God.

Go in business for yourself. If someone's ministry really challenges you, it should make you seek God for yourself, not follow him around feeding second-hand on his revelations.

There is nothing wrong with attending conferences and seminars, but if what you get there is not changing you, there *is* something wrong. If you think by following some minister around but not seeking God for yourself will enable you to make spiritual growth, you are badly mistaken.

If you are where you were spiritually five years ago, you have been hard-headed and probably have the wrong attitude about changing yourself to the image of Jesus.

If you do not want to be a mediocre Christian, begin to exercise. Your fellowship with God must be personal, not second-hand. You cannot rest on your parents' experience, your pastor's experience, or some great evangelist's experience.

You must have your own fellowship with the Father, just as you must have your own relationship.

None of those people can be born again for you, nor can they build a fellowship with God for you. The flow of power through you comes from fellowshipping with the Holy Spirit. You need power to put the devil on the run.

Do you want God really to use you? Then stop acting like a Gabby-Hayes character in the old westerns. He always showed his little badge, but the hero did all the work. That is all some Christians are doing, showing the devil their badges but not knocking off any bad guys.

Coming to Grips With the Devil

You must come to grips with the reality of demonic oppression and possession before you can fight demons. I remember being a seven or eight year old in school and knowing a guy that I was really afraid of. And he looked at me and knew I was afraid.

He talked about me and had all the little girls laughing at me, and all the fellows knew. Once as he was moving away from me, I became really provoked and picked up a half-brick to throw at him. I did not even aim but just tossed that thing — and it hit him right in the middle of the back!

He said, "Ouch!" Then he turned around and started at me, and I started to run. When I got even with a sand box on the playground, suddenly something rose up in me.

I said, "I'm not going to run anymore," so I turned around and waited on him.

Now I had not come to grips with the situation when I was standing there afraid. I had not come to grips with it when I threw the brick even, nor had I come to grips with it when I ran. When I stopped, and we got into a clench is when I finally came to grips with that problem.

When you let something run you, it is getting the best of you. Only when you stop and take hold of it do you have a chance of beating it. When you tell that thing you are not running any longer, when you make a stand, then you are coming to grips with it.

Coming to grips means "to squeeze, to hold tight, to clench." That is what addicts go through. They can purpose in their heart to beat this thing that has them bound, they can talk about quitting all they want to. But only when they admit they are hooked and seek help are they coming to grips with their addictions.

Jacob, son of Isaac and grandson of Abraham, ran from his brother Esau and was afraid for his life for almost twenty years. He knew he had cheated his twin brother when he conned him out of the birthright, and he knew Esau had vowed to kill him. All of those years he worked for his Uncle Laban in a distant country, he could put that fear and apprehension out of his mind.

However, it did not go away, because it had not been dealt with. Finally, he was heading back home with his wives, maidservants, and eleven children, plus all of the wealth he had gained. Now life was catching up with him.

The last night before meeting up with Esau, Jacob came to grips with his problem. (Gen. 32.) He was tired of nightmares about his brother seeking to kill him. He probably had times when he woke up in the middle of the night in a cold sweat. Now Esau was on the other side of the river with four hundred men.

Jacob was facing a crisis. A crisis is a time when you have reached your limits on something. You are in a state of emergency. Everything in you is crying S.O.S. You feel that you are "between the devil and the deep blue sea."

The Israelites got to that place when they were camped between Pharoah's army and the Red Sea. That is what you call a crisis. You have reached a crossroads of some kind, and the stress and conflict within becomes greater than the conflict without. That is a time of crisis.

When you have used up all your resources, and you do not know where to get strength or help, you are in a crisis. You cannot go any farther, and you do not know what to tell God that you have not already told Him. The bottom has seemingly dropped out of everything. That is where Jacob was when he reached Peniel on his way home.

Genesis 32:24 says that Jacob was left alone, and that is where you have to be in order to come to grips with something. It must be just you and the Holy Spirit facing the devil. Spiritual warfare begins with an individual coming to grips with something. Even when it is a corporate warfare, whatever group is involved must come together in such unity that the people become as *one* person facing the enemy.

On the Day of Pentecost, Luke wrote that the one hundred and twenty people who were tarrying (fasting and praying) for the Holy Spirit to come were *in one accord*. (Acts 2:1.) Until they became in one accord, I do not believe the Comforter could come, because there were (and still are) certain conditions we must meet for Him to exercise His power.

Jacob came to grips with his old nature — the trickster, the sneaky behavior — when he wrestled all night with an angel at Peniel. (Gen. 32:24-32.) I do not believe any man is strong enough to wrestle all night with an angel. I believe Jacob had times during the night when he just held on until he got his second wind.

There is nothing a mortal man can do with an angel, but Jacob wrestled, held on, and stood his ground. He stopped being wimpy and trying to get things in underhanded ways. For possibly the first time in his life, he met a crisis head on and determined to win the victory.

Seven things happened to Jacob there:

1. His name was changed. From "trickster, usurper, supplanter," he became *Israel,* "one who rules as God."1 (vv. 27,28.)

2. He prevailed and was blessed. (vv. 25,28.)

3. He met God face to face. (v. 30.)

4. His life was preserved. (v. 30.)

5. The sun rose upon him. (v. 31.) When you come to grips with a thing, and purpose in your heart that you are going to win in Jesus' name, day will break through the night of darkness you have been in.

6. He was able to face what he had come to grips with. (Gen. 33:1-3.) He left limping, having met God face to face, and went to meet Esau without fear. The thing he had feared had lost its power over him. When they met, instead of fighting, tears came to their eyes. They threw their arms around one another and fell on one another's neck.

7. Jacob humbled himself. He bowed before Esau seven times. (Gen. 33:3.) Then they offered gifts to one another.

The Bible does not tell us if Esau still held a grudge. If he did, it disappeared at that meeting. Some time later, because Israel had so many cattle and sheep, Esau even moved his family and herds farther away so there would be no friction. (Gen. 36:6,7.)

Sometimes in coming to grips with something, you must face master demons. If you do not know how to fight, choose your ground, and just grit your teeth and hang on. Keep reminding yourself that the devil already has been spoiled. Yes, he is real, demons are real, and they have power. *But* you have more power, and you have authority. They are operating illegally.

---

[1]Strong, James. "Hebrew and Chaldee Dictionary," *The New Strong's Exhaustive Concordance of the Bible* (Nashville: Thomas Nelson Publishers, 1984), p. 53, #3478.

7

Satan Has Been Spoiled

Satan has been spoiled, and the word *spoiled* means "damaged, robbed of good things, ruined, impaired, decayed, wasted, injured," and so forth. To sum up: It means *defeated!*

How do we know that? We know it because the Word of God specifically says that. We are not left to interpret, infer, or guess at it. The Apostle Paul spelled it out for us, as he did so many other things. He gave answers to deep theological questions before the Church even had the questions. Look at Colossians 2:9-15:

> For in him dwelleth all the fulness of the Godhead bodily.
>
> And ye are complete in him, which is the head of all principality and power:
>
> In whom also ye are circumcised with the circumcision made without hands, in putting off the body of the sins of the flesh by the circumcision of Christ:
>
> Buried with him in baptism, wherein also ye are risen with him through the faith of the operation of God, who hath raised him from the dead.
>
> And you, being dead in your sins and the uncircumcision of your flesh, hath he quickened together with him, having forgiven you all trespasses;

> Blotting out the handwriting of ordinances that was against us, which was contrary to us, and took it out of the way, nailing it to his cross;
>
> And having *spoiled* principalities and powers, he made a shew of them openly, triumphing over them in it.

You may say that Satan is not mentioned there, only his chief demons or fallen angels. However, Jesus could not have spoiled them without spoiling Satan. He said that Himself:

> Or else how can one enter into a strong man's house, and *spoil* his goods, except he first bind the strong man? and then he will spoil his house.
>
> Matthew 12:29

The same comment of Jesus was recorded in Mark 3:27, and Luke 11:21,22 makes it even plainer.

> When a strong man armed keepeth his palace, his goods are in peace:
>
> But when a stronger than he shall come upon him, and overcome him, he taketh from him all his armour wherein he trusted, and divideth his *spoils.*

Isaiah had prophesied this hundreds of years before:

> Therefore will I divide him a portion with the great, and he shall divide the *spoil* with the strong; because he hath poured out his soul unto death: and he was numbered with the transgressors; and he bare the sin of many, and made intercession for the transgressors.
>
> Isaiah 53:12

Then Paul wrote in Philippians that God had given Jesus a name above every name, one to which everything in the *heavens, earth,* and *under the earth* should bow. When God says *everything,* He means nothing is left out. He said *every* tongue would confess that Jesus is Lord. (Philip. 2:9-11.)

Jesus came to defeat the works of Satan, John wrote. (1 John 3:8.) And He could not defeat Satan's works without defeating him. He could not defeat him and leave his angels and demons unspoiled. Therefore, on the cross, Jesus defeated Satan and all of his followers.

We read about the crucifixion and see how humiliated Jesus was. We see how He suffered from beatings, thorns pressed into His head, and a sword stuck into His side. Mary's firstborn Son, hanging naked in front of all passers by, treated like a common criminal when He had never done anything.

As sad as that is, and as much as we should appreciate that, we are only seeing what happened in the natural. In the Spirit realm, something much different was occurring. While they were nailing Him to the cross, He was nailing all of the ordinances against us to the cross.

That is why the devil is so angry. Before Jesus came, and he made the mistake of instigating His death, Satan had dominion over the earth. He originated all of its systems. In the beginning, he and his "heads of state" could openly walk on earth. All of the old gods and goddesses from Chaldea down to Rome, Greece, and Europe, are based on fallen angels or demonic powers who came to earth and demanded worship and sacrifices.

The statues of characters that history calls "myths" were real demons and demonic personalities.

After Jesus came, all Satan can do is what we, the Church, allow him to do. The main thing to remember is that we are dealing with a wounded adversary. One of the worst things a hunter can face is a wounded large animal — moose, bear, or tiger. When they are wounded, they are more vicious. The pain makes them angry. They know man is the cause of it, and they will attack to the point of death once they are wounded. Also, their pain and frustration will be taken out on anything around.

Satan is losing all the way around. He has excelled in nothing. Also, there is no hope for him. There is no way he can repent, even if he wanted to. There is no way made for redemption for Satan and other angelic beings. One reason is that they had no right to choose. The Creator made them to serve Him in various ways, and they are not made in His image. He gave them no right to decide anything for themselves. Once they made choices, and those choices were against Him, they were doomed.

Man had the right to choose, so even when he chose wrongly, God could make a way back for him. There is no way back for the devil. Satan knows already he is doomed. He knows his destiny.

Put the Devil Where He Belongs

We have already seen that the devil belongs under our feet, but you cannot put him where he belongs if you are not where *you* belong. Ephesians 1:20-24, which I have already quoted, shows us where Jesus is — at God's right hand in Heaven.

In the very next chapter, Paul writes about where we are *positionally*. (That means by right, but not yet literally.)

> **And hath raised us up together, and made us sit together in heavenly places in Christ Jesus.**
> **Ephesians 2:6**

Ephesians 1:3 says that God has blessed us with all spiritual blessings in heavenly places. In Hebrews 7:26, Jesus is called our high priest who is *higher* than the heavens.

Paul also said that God had given Jesus to be head over all things to the Church, which is His Body. From the spiritual aspect, Jesus and His Church are *one*. As the Head, He is supposed to be directing things. As the Body, we ought to be following orders and moving in the direction the Head turns.

Sadly enough, we are not doing that. We are like a person with multiple sclerosis or a palsy of some kind. Instead of operating in unity and obedience to the Head, we are sort of spastic, different branches going off in various directions.

No wonder the devil does not stay under our feet where he belongs. The Church is not to be an organization but an *organism*. An *organization* is something put together in the natural, functioning as best it can with very diverse people trying to run it. An *organism* is something whole and integrated, and something *alive*.

The quicker we stop fighting one another, the quicker we can begin to operate in authority and power, the quicker we can truly represent Jesus on earth.

Ever know a head to sit down without a body? When Jesus ascended and sat down at the Father's right hand, that is where we are supposed to be in the Spirit. If we were truly "seated" where we ought to be, the devil would be where he ought to be.

Ephesians 4:8 says that when Jesus ascended, He led captivity captive and gave gifts to men. He that ascended, Paul wrote, is also He that first descended into the lower parts of the earth. Jesus did that in order to fulfill all of God's purposes and plans.

Jesus had to go to the lowest parts and the highest parts to fulfill all things. If we are Christ's body and seated in heavenly places, that puts us above the devil. No, that does not mean you will have no trials or tribulations. That does not mean the devil is not going to try to afflict you, torment you, harass you, and antagonize you.

What it does mean, however, is that once you know where *you* belong and where *he* belongs, it will be much easier to keep him there. When you do not realize where you belong, you really do not know who you are. You do not know your rights and privileges in Christ, much less your responsibilities.

Spiritual warfare is one of your responsibilities, just like getting people saved, healed, and matured. When you rise up and walk in your rightful place, you will be able to look at your present circumstances as a stepping stone to the next place God wants you to be.

Afflictions, tests, trials, sicknesses, and other things come, but because I know my place and I know the devil's place, I walk above them, not under them. I take dominion over circumstances and over the devil. Start taking advantage of your authority.

Remember that the Lord is on your side. According to the scriptures we have already looked at, we are over the devil. If you want to stay in that place and keep him under your feet, you must hold your ground.

You overcome by holding your ground and taking more territory back from the enemy. In Revelation, John said the saints overcame by the blood of the Lamb and the word of their testimony. If you win no battles over Satan, you have no testimony. On the other hand, if you do win a battle and testify about it, you may have to fight to hang onto your testimony. The devil does not give up easily.

When you testify, the devil will fight you. But when you win that victory, you have won two. Each victory helps. Each victory over the devil gives you confidence and strengthens you.

Seven Ways To Keep the Devil Underfoot

I have written about the weapons given us by God to keep the devil underfoot, but now I want to take another look at some of them.

Fasting is the first way. Fasting frees you from oppression. Sometimes you can look free on the outside, but be in spiritual bonds on the inside.

God spoke to Isaiah about the purpose of fasting:

> **Is not this the fast that I have chosen? to loose the bands of wickedness, to undo the heavy burdens, and to let the oppressed go free, and that ye break every yoke?**
>
> **Is it not to deal thy bread to the hungry, and that thou bring the poor that are cast out to thy house? when thou seest the naked, that thou cover him; and that thou hide not thyself from thine own flesh?**
> **Isaiah 58:6,7**

The verses that precede these talk about how the religious people were fasting: "for strife and argument, to get their own way, for their own pleasure and purposes, to look righteous." (Isa. 58:3-5.)

Jesus also rebuked the Pharisees of His day for their attitudes about fasting. (Matt. 6:16-18.) So you can see that the purpose and attitude with which you go into fasting are as important as fasting itself. Also, you need to use some wisdom about fasting, or your weapon will backfire.

If your head hurts, your stomach hurts, and other areas hurt, those are signs you need to fast for the body's sake. Those reactions show there are a lot of toxic poisons in your system and not clearing them out will obscure your spiritual purposes. Clean your system *before* you fast, and you will be able to truly accomplish your spiritual purpose.

Poisons collect in the colon, the garbage can of the body. That needs to be cleaned out in order for you really to be able to fast. Then, usually after the third or fourth day, hunger leaves and strength will begin to return.

If you are planning a lengthy fast, it is a good idea to take two or three days to clean out your system with juices before you start the real fast. That will flush out the poisons. Use as natural a product as you can to flush out your system.

The second way to defeat the devil is *prevailing prayer*. That does not mean crawling into bed and mumbling, "Now I lay me down to sleep." Prevailing prayer is when you get down on your face or knees and stay there until you know you have "prayed through." The devil does not like for you to pray.

The third way to keep him underfoot is with *the Word of God*. The only way to use the Bible against the devil is to have it hidden in your heart. If you know none of the Word, you cannot use it, and if you quote it with no more power or belief than good poetry, for example, it will not accomplish its purpose.

When the Word is in your heart, it is part of you, and when things happen, it will just roll up out of your spirit full of power and authority. The Word is especially important as a weapon when the devil fights you in your own mind.

He will come to you and whisper that God does not love you, that no one loves you, or that your husband or wife is cheating on you — all sorts of lies. God said that, although a mother may forget her child, He will not forget us.

He said that we are engraved on the palms of His hands. (Isa. 49:14-16.) Times like these are when you need to quote the Word to yourself. Edify yourself with the Word. That will stop the devil from messing with your head. Encourage yourself with the Word in your prayer life.

If the devil tries to take something in your life — health, marriage, job, or whatever — tell him he did not give it to you, and he has no right to take it away. Tell him "it is written," and then read him the right act from the Bible.

The fourth way to keep the devil underfoot is *the name of Jesus*. This actually is the quickest way to get the devil off of you. For example, as soon as you feel symptoms of the flu or anything else, begin to come against the devil with the name that is above every name.

Do not wait until your head is hurting, your nose is running, and your stomach is upset. Begin at the first hint of trouble. It is very difficult to rebuke him off of you after whatever he is putting on you gets a good hold on your body.

As soon as you suspect something has been thrown at you, begin to say, "Satan, I rebuke you in the name of Jesus. It is written that you have to bow your knee to that name. It is above every name on earth."

You must learn how to nip things in the bud. Start your day with Jesus, and end your day with Jesus. Go to sleep in an atmosphere of praising the Lord and calling the name of Jesus. When you get to the point that you truly understand what it means to you, that name of Jesus will be precious in your mind.

The use of the name of Jesus actually goes hand in hand with the fifth way to defeat Satan: *rejoicing in the Lord.*

When you truly rejoice, you have joy, joy, joy down in your heart. You feel uplifted. When you feel uplifted, you can work better. You can pray better. You feel stronger physically, as well as spiritually. Christians ought to be the happiest people on earth.

Jesus said to rejoice even when men revile and persecute you, when people lie against you. Why would He say that? Jesus promised that your reward will be great in Heaven if that happens, because the world persecuted the prophets before you. In other words, rejoice! You are in good company. Do not let the devil get you down by causing people to lie about you. Rejoice!

You can always find something to rejoice about, things like your salvation, your healing, eternal life with God. If you try, you can think of many things to rejoice over. When we are happy in our spirits, we can judge situations better and handle things better.

As a matter of fact, if you do not set yourself to come to church rejoicing, the devil will have a chance to steal the Word from you before you get home. When you come to church burdened, weighed down with cares and weights, you are not coming to worship God or to meet the Holy Spirit.

A merry heart not only defeats the devil and praises God, but it does you good like a medicine. (Prov. 17:22.)

The sixth and seventh ways to defeat Satan are found in Revelation 12:11. They also were discussed in the chapter on weapons. But I want to give you some more ideas on overcoming through the blood of Jesus and the word of your testimony.

I heard a holiness preacher say once that the blood of Jesus was no different from any other man's! All I could do was pray that God would forgive him. The blood of Jesus *was* different from every other man's. That is the whole point of His shedding His blood — because it was not like the rest of mankind's.

Adam's blood became poisoned with toxic sin and disobedience, and every other man *but Jesus* inherited the blood of Adam. It is so important to plead the blood of Jesus over your children and other family members.

Abel's blood cried out to God from the ground (Gen. 4:10), and if human blood is that powerful, how much more powerful the blood of Jesus. His blood cries out from the cross, not for vengeance, but for atonement. If the blood of a lamb was powerful enough to keep the death angel away from the Israelites' homes in Egypt (Ex. 12:21-23), how much more powerful is the blood of Jesus? (Heb. 9:13,14,19-28)

God very specifically said to the Israelites that *the life of everything is in the blood.* (Lev. 17:11.) Every person has a time to die (Eccle. 3:2), but pleading the blood of Jesus can help you remain on earth as long as God intends. Blood saved the Israelites from the death angel.

You need to keep your eyes on the fact that it is Jesus who is the source of your salvation. If you make the mistake of letting the blood become like a "magic potion" to you or a "talisman," you will open the door to Satan, not close it. There are a number of cults that make a fetish out of the blood of Jesus. Your hope must be in Him, and His blood is a weapon *because of what it did and what it stands for.*

I was rebuking death off someone once in a guest bedroom in my home, and I saw the spirit of death. This lady was staying at my home when she had some sort of attack.

The spirit of death was so black that even the whites of his eyes looked dirty. He had on a white shirt, but it looked as if he had been in a coal mine. He was filthy and had a hump back. He carried a sack, and it was dirty. His eyes were red, and the palms of his hands were black.

I rebuked him until I won that fight. However, he looked at me just as plain and said, ''I'm gone — but I'll be back.''

He left, but sure enough, they took this person for whom I was praying to the hospital, and death soon came and took her away. However, death is not an enemy to the saints. Jesus defeated death's sting (1 Cor. 15:55), Paul wrote. To the believer, death is simply a door to the beginning of their *real* lives.

You do not want to be cheated out of doing everything on earth that God wants you to do, however. As I saw him, death was short and not very big, but until he is put under the feet of Jesus as the last enemy (1 Cor. 15:26), he is very powerful.

I was going through something years ago, and a sister in the Lord saw a vision about it. She saw me wrestling with a little black dwarf, and he was giving me a hard time. He was throwing me, and I was throwing him, when suddenly strength came to me. I could feel the anointing of the Lord. Death is mighty, but God is Almighty.

Death comes in many forms. Because I have seen him this way does not mean he would look like that to you. Demons can transform themselves into other shapes. However, no matter what they look like, they are what they are. As I began to rebuke him, I could feel cold chills. Your body reacts to the presence of a supernatural being.

Whether it is death or any other demon, put it under your feet. That is where the devil belongs. To do that, you will have to ignore the body and ignore the thoughts that your mind throws up. Simply find which weapon is the right one for the situation, and set out to win!

8

Lord, Make Me a Terror to the Enemy

Every Christian today should be praying, "Lord, make me a terror to the enemy."

For a long time, I have been praying this and claiming it. I have seen very clearly how serious the battle is and what is involved.

Years ago, another preacher said to me, even before I began to pastor a church, "Henton, you are a fighter."

And, of course, that is my calling. I am called to make the Body aware of the need for spiritual warfare and to train as many other fighters as I can. I realize that not everyone is called to the same ministry. Some are called to preach faith, some to preach salvation, and some to demonstrate the gifts of the Spirit. However, no matter what your calling, at some point, you will have to move into spiritual warfare to continue to win the victory.

Believers who are not set in any of the fivefold offices will have to face the enemy in their private lives. Naturally, he has it in for me, because I am revealing his tricks, his snares, his purposes, his motives — even, to some people, his very existence. However, he also is after those who are not exposing him, simply because they are deputies of Jesus.

Of course, there will be times when you will not know right offhand whether something is of God or the devil. That may sound odd, but we do not always know when something is for our good. And I am not talking about sickness, disease, or poverty. You can know God is not in anything that He does not have. None of those things, no crimes or wickedness, come from God.

So if someone runs out in front of you and tries to kill you — it is not God doing it. If you get hit with cancer, you can know right off it is not God. If fear suddenly paralyzes you in a situation — it has to be the devil. God's warnings about danger come with a peace that cannot be mistaken.

Confusion and chaos are not of God. So you see there are some clear-cut situations where you immediately know to begin coming against the devil with the Word, the name of Jesus, and the blood of Jesus. If someone tries to break up your marriage, light in on the devil!

However, suppose you have a flat tire on the way to the airport. How are you going to know right off if an angel is stopping you from getting on a plane that will crash, killing everyone on board, or if the devil is trying to hinder you?

Sometimes, you can get a clear witness in your spirit as to which it is. Other times, you have to see the consequences or the results in order to know. Either way, if you do not let the devil cause you to lose your joy over it, he has not won. Go on to the airport and catch the next plane.

You may say, "That's going too far, Pastor, asking to be made a terror to the devil. I don't want the devil to be scared of me."

I say it is about time for some demons to become afraid of some Christians! They have been running the lives of far too many of us. We must learn the art of defending ourselves. How long does the devil have to run over you before you get angry and do something about it?

We need to learn a lesson from Jesus' words in Matthew 11:12:

> **And from the days of John the Baptist until now the kingdom of heaven suffereth violence, and the violent take it by force.**

The word *violence* in that verse is the Greek word *biazo*, which means "to force, or to crowd oneself into."[1] From the time John began to call the Jews to repentance and baptize them, many of the residents of Judea had eagerly sought the Kingdom of Heaven.

Violent also means "earnestness, toughness, forcefulness, and intense striving." Watch those people who tell you that you do not have to do anything in the Kingdom but lay back and watch God work. In some instances, you lay back, and the devil will run over you. He will flatten you while you are laying back.

We have a great increase today in people trying to take the world by violence. They are striving, breaking laws, even hurting other people. That is a perversion of the eagerness that would press in strongly to be part of the Kingdom of God.

Everything to do with the devil is: bind it, loose it, break it, destroy it, or cast it out. We understand "binding and loosing," and we understand "casting out" something. But how about break and destroy where the devil is concerned?

Break means "to knock apart, to fracture, to damage, to weaken, to interrupt." Notice that the yoke of bondage will be destroyed by the anointing. (Isa. 10:27.) *Destroy* means "to make useless, to ruin beyond repair, to make an end to something, to demolish something." Some yokes are to be broken, and some are to be destroyed.

It Is time To Get Angry at the Devil

To run the devil out of our homes and neighborhoods, we are going to have to get violent about it. We are going to have to let a holy violence rise up in us. We tend to think all anger is wrong, but there is an anger which is "righteous indignation." That is anger on behalf of the Kingdom of God. When Jesus ran the moneychangers out of the temple, He was expressing righteous indignation. (Matt. 21:12,13.)

Anger is a degree of intensity and can be constructive as well as negative. Demons will work to get us mad at one another.

They will drop these kinds of thoughts in your mind, "They're talking about you. Don't you see them looking at each other and whispering? Sister So-and-so did not speak to you in church this morning."

The devil gets us mad at one another. Soon we are fighting one another. This does not just happen to people, but to denominations, various movements of God, and even local churches. Within churches, the devil loves to stir things up and cause church splits.

Then the demon stands back and snickers at us, "Look at them! They are saving us the trouble. They are fighting and destroying one another. Why in the world does God love them, when they are so stupid?"

Love casts out fear (1 John 4:18), and so does anger. If you are afraid of demons, get mad at them. Get angry at what they are doing to your marriage, your family, and society. When you get angry, your Adrenalin rises. When you get angry at the devil, your spiritual Adrenalin rises.

You will be surprised what you can do when you step out in faith, when you become willing to fight a good warfare. A lot of times, we are talking to God when we need to be speaking to the devil.

Moses was worried that he was not equal to the task of bringing the Israelites out of Egypt. (Ex. 4:1,10.)

And God said, "Why are you crying to Me? Use your authority. I gave you that rod. Stretch out your hand and use it." (Ex. 4:2.)

God's anger was kindled against Moses, because He had given him orders and weapons. Moses was to do his assignment in God's might, not his own. I can almost hear God saying some similar things to us today:

> And Moses said unto the Lord, O my Lord, I am not eloquent, neither heretofore, nor since thou hast spoken unto thy servant: but I am slow of speech, and of a slow tongue.

> And the Lord said unto him, Who hath made man's mouth? or who maketh the dumb, or deaf, or the seeing, or the blind? have not I the Lord?

> Now therefore go, and I will be with thy mouth, and teach thee what thou shalt say.

> And he said, O my Lord, send, I pray thee, by the hand of him whom thou wilt send.

And the anger of the Lord was kindled against Moses . . . . (But God relented and sent Aaron to speak for Moses.)

Exodus 4:10-14

I feel God is saying to us:

"Who made your mouths? Who has given you the weapons? Have I not promised to be with you and never leave you?"

Moses was one of the greatest heroes of the Bible, but he started out as timid as any Christian today who has never been involved in spiritual warfare. After he moved out in the work of the Lord, he gained boldness and became one of the greatest spiritual warriors of all time.

He became so angry and shocked at the Israelites' idolatry at Mt. Sinai that he dropped the tablets of the law. And he carried out God's judgment when it was necessary.

Anger is a strong impetus to fight. If you get angry enough, you can fight and not know you are hurt. I understand pit bulls are like that. Where dog fights are legal, they use pit bulls a lot, because they get angry and fight for three or four hours, no matter how badly they are injured.

When you get tired enough of the devil whipping you around, you will get angry at him. You will begin to take the Kingdom by force. You will get violent in the spiritual realm. You take after the devil with that righteous indignation, and pretty soon, the anointing will come. We need the anointing to whip the devil.

The Anointing Brings Deliverance

Years ago, saints *worked* to bring souls into the Kingdom. They worked at the altar to defeat demons.

Those old sisters would pray you through under a strong anointing. When they let up, you knew something had happened. A lot of demons would just leave people during all of that prevailing prayer.

We do not have altar workers like that anymore. Sometimes during revivals, workers were at the altar until three or four in the morning. They may not have known a whole lot about the Bible, but they knew Jesus saved. They knew the anointing, and they knew prayer.

They were pulling demons out of people. When someone was saved at those altars, they were *changed*. We need more times like those today. Those old sisters were terrors to the devil.

The Apostle Paul was a terror to the devil. Those demons that whipped the sons of Sceva put Paul in the same category as Jesus. They *knew* those two well. Any time the devil does not know you, you are in trouble, because you are not doing anything for God. You can expect no rewards in Heaven.

Demons operate as "follow-up committees," I believe. Let someone get saved, and here comes his old girlfriend, a drinking buddy, or someone he used to do drugs with. All of them immediately try to pull him back into sin. But if you get saved and settle down to just warm a pew, they kind of put you on the back burner.

The devil's follow-up committee is more diligent and faithful than those in our churches. They do not send a convert a card, "Glad to see you at church." They do not just call and tell you how everyone missed you at church, when you are not there. The devil's committees send someone to drag the new convert back out to the night clubs.

We need to become as angry at the devil as Samson finally was at the Philistines. But for the first part of his life, Samson was like many Christians are today. He played games with the enemy, because he was overconfident. And he wanted to be God's man but still have the sinful pleasures of the Philistines. He compromised his calling.

On the other hand, when Samson was following God's way in the natural realm, he was everything Jesus was in the spiritual realm. When Samson walked in the strength of the Lord, nothing could stop him. Jesus *always walked in the strength of the Lord,* and nothing in the spiritual realm could stop Him.

Samson destroyed more of the enemy by his death than during his lifetime — so did Jesus.

Nothing could stand up to Samson, as long as he obeyed God; nothing stood up to Jesus His entire lifetime, because He *did* obey the Father. God anointed Jesus, who went about doing good, the Word says. Nothing could stand before Him.

Samson killed a thousand Philistines with the jawbone of a donkey once. (Judg. 15:15-17.) When you have that holy violence and know you are called to a certain purpose, you can do phenomenal things.

That is why Christians today need to find out for sure that they are called to bust the heads of demons. Then they need to become very angry at the devil. They need to be filled with spiritual Adrenalin, so that we can take the Kingdom by force. We can, with eagerness, move into doing a good warfare on behalf of the Kingdom.

We must know as never before that God is looking for spiritual "daredevils." He is not looking for "grandstanders," people showing off. Just as God said to Joshua about the giants of his day, "Not a man shall stand before you" (Josh. 1:5), He is saying that to us today.

He is saying, "Church, stretch out your rod of authority. I have called you to lead people out of bondage. Not a demon shall stand before you, if you have the courage to move out and fulfill My purposes. Use your own 'jawbone' against the enemy: speak forth My Word. That will defeat them."

I would hope that those who read this book will be encouraged and challenged into beginning to exercise their spiritual weapons in a determination to fight the good fight of faith and defeat many demons.

I pray that many readers will be saying: "Lord, make me a terror to the devil!"

---

[1]Strong, James. "Greek Dictionary of the New Testament," *The New Strong's Exhaustive Concordance of the Bible* (Nashville: Thomas Nelson Publishers, 1984), p.19, #971.

About the Author

Evangelist Richard Daniel Henton founded Monument of Faith Evangelical Church in Chicago, Illinois, in 1964. Through his leadership, the once-small congregation has grown to numbers in excess of three thousand members and is still growing steadily.

In 1948, at the age of fifteen and while still in high school, Evangelist Henton clearly heard God's call to enter the ministry. The Lord's call was loud and clear, reaching the depth of his soul. He therefore began preaching the gospel of Christ.

After being called to the ministry, Evangelist Henton diligently studied the Bible and engaged himself in fasting and prayer, which is the foundation of his ministry.

Having evangelized more than thirty years extensively throughout the United States, the dynamic, multi-faceted ministry has touched the lives of men and women everywhere. His great crusades have witnessed scores of men and women saved and filled with the Holy Spirit.